# the

# TEEN

# self-esteem

# WORKBOOK

## 8 Power Ups to Overcome your Insecurities and Boost your Confidence and Self-Worth.

# the TEEN

## self-esteem
## WORKBOOK

8 Power Ups to Overcome your Insecurities and Boost your Confidence and Self-Worth.

# Medical Disclaimer

This book does not contain medical [medical referring to mental and physical health throughout his disclaimer] and health advice. The health information contained in this book is provided for general information and educational purposes only and is not intended as and shall not be understood or construed as professional medical advice, diagnosis or treatment, or substitute for professional medical advice, diagnosis or treatment.
Before taking any action based upon such information, we expressly recommend that you seek advice from medical professionals.

Your use of the book including the implementation of any suggestions or recommendations laid out in the book does not create a doctor-patient relationship.

Your use of the book is solely at your own risk and you expressly agree not to rely upon any information contained in the book as a substitute for professional medical advice, diagnosis or treatment.

Under no circumstances shall Teen Thrive be held liable or responsible for any errors or omissions in the book or for any damage you may suffer with respect to any actions taken or not taken based on any or all of the contents of the book. and/ or as a result of failing to seek competent advice from medical professionals.

"Whether it is used independently or in conjunction with psychotherapy, this book is a powerful tool to build self-esteem in teens!"

"...By far the best self-esteem workbook I have read, and admittedly, I learned a few new techniques."

"The Teen Self-Esteem Workbook" by Teen Thrive should serve as the go-to standard for teens and teen advocates."

"I've never come across anything like it, and I found it to be refreshing, enlightening, and enjoyable."

*need a boost to get you started on your daily gratitude practice?*

CLAIM YOUR FREE

# positivity card deck

SCAN ME

FOR DUDES

for girls

# TABLE OF CONTENTS
## FOR SELF-ESTEEM WORKBOOK:

# TABLE OF CONTENTS
## FOR SELF-ESTEEM WORKBOOK:

# FOREWARD

## by Dr. Crystal Burwell

The Teen Self-Esteem Workbook by Teen Thrive is engaging, empowering and interactive. The workbook is an incredible resource for teens and adults. As a psychotherapist in private practice and former director of adolescent programs, I'm well acquainted with the challenges teens face. In my clinical work, I'm constantly reminding teens to work on their most important relationship- their relationship with themselves.

One of my favorite quotes begs the question, "If I asked you to name all the things you love, how long would it take for you to name yourself?"

Too often, I work with teens and adults unable to answer this question. My job is to serve as their therapeutic GPS, guiding them along the way. Therapists, teachers, parents, and teen advocates have the awesome responsibility of facilitating individuation and self-agency in the lives of young people. Teens are counting on us to model healthy behaviors and create safe spaces for growth.

If you are reading this right now and are going through your teenage years, chances are you are struggling to find a solid sense of self. Remember this, on your journey of self-discovery, your first stop is self-esteem- loving yourself for who you are! Without this foundation, you'll more than likely experience a failure to launch, grow, and thrive.

"The Teen Self-Esteem Workbook" explores eight different "Power-Ups," symbolized by a personal map. Each destination targets a component of self-esteem and guides you along your developmental journey toward improved self-esteem. Each Power-Up helps you construct a personalized plan to navigate each challenge.

The Teen Self-Esteem Workbook by Teen Thrive explores areas such as healthy relationships, family life, and school success. The overall goal is to identify areas of life that need more attention. Equipped with this information, you'll be prepared to travel the uncharted terrain of adolescence.

As a practitioner, I really love that the workbook design allows for independent or collaborative use, which means that you can use it on your own or within a therapeutic setting. In addition to being useful, the workbook is interesting, attractive, and fun! With each power-up, you'll be building the mental fortitude and resilience you need to weather any storm. While other workbooks are disengaging and boring, this workbook guides you on a reflective journey toward growth.

The Teen Self-Esteem Workbook by Teen Thrive should serve as the go-to standard for teens and teen advocates.

I encourage you to read through this workbook and really think about the exercises. It will help you find your tribe, harness your strengths, and affirm your ability to do hard things. You'll discover how to think critically, own your stories, and set your own course. Despite plot twists and turns, you'll be prepared for success as you navigate the journey of a lifetime.

Oh, the places you'll go!

Crystal Burwell, Ph.D, LPC, CPCS
Owner & Psychotherapist
Dr. Burwell Speaks, LLC

# WELCOME

To the Teen Self-Esteem Workbook.
It is great to have you here.

**As you open this book, try to notice what you're feeling.**

## EXCITEMENT?
## APPREHENSION?
## AN URGE TO ROLL YOUR EYES?

It's fine if you do. It's never been easy to be a teenager, but it's particularly challenging now. We know that teens today are experiencing rising levels of anxiety, depression, and even FOMO (fear of missing out), but I don't need to bore you with all of that information - you already know it.

In spite of it all,

you have many reasons for optimism.

If you're opening this book, that means you already have a strong support system of people that want to see you succeed (by the way, your support system doesn't have to be perfect because it won't be), you possess self-compassion, and upon completion of the book, you will have the skills and insight to move forward in a healthier way.

# The Eight Power-Ups in this workbook are a comprehensive way to improve self-esteem.

While it can feel like there are countless things to worry about on a daily basis, if we can focus on one Power Up at a time and identify our priorities, we are inevitably setting ourselves up for success. But, like anything else, it takes patience, practice, and plenty of failures.

I'm talking about constant failure. Big failure. Small failure. All of it.

I'm guessing you weren't expecting to read the word "failure" so many times in a book about self-esteem, were you? Well, failure is a big part of becoming an adult and, surprisingly, improving self-esteem. One of my favorite quotes comes from a psychologist named Dr. Claire Weeks:

"Strength is not born from strength. Strength can be born only from weakness. So be glad of your weaknesses now; they are the beginnings of your strength."

Maybe you're not the best student, you don't feel very confident in your body, or social media (looking at you, Instagram) makes you feel low. Overcoming these very fears is ultimately what will lead to empowerment. But that seems daunting - so how do we do that?

As you work your way through the 8 Power-Ups, try to be mindful of when you feel like you're failing or when you're reading about something that makes you experience fear. We can be both afraid and approach that fearful thought with curiosity. We can practice self-compassion and acknowledge how much time it can take to make meaningful change. Too often, we live life in the black & white - the all-or-nothing. We declare things a success or a failure.

In reality, the only way to live a healthy life is to live in the gray—the in-between.

And how do we do that? By embracing our imperfections. As you work your way through the book, remember this quote by J. Cole:

## "We ain't picture perfect, but we're worth the picture still."

You will always be worth the picture, no matter how messy it can get. Best of luck on your journey -

I believe in you.

Fred Kutnick, LCSW
Anxiety & Trauma Therapist,
Practicing in New York, NY

# OK, LET'S GET STARTED

## What is self esteem?

What is self-esteem? You may hear the term thrown around a lot. Maybe you will learn about it in school. It might be a topic that flashes up on social media. You might hear about it in the news. It might even come up with your friends.

Self-esteem is all about how you feel about yourself--your looks, your personality, and how you think about how your life is going right now. Many things influence your self-esteem, including:

**Peer pressure**

**Comparision**

**Trends**

**Wanting to fit in**

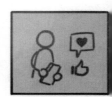
**Social Media**

Overwhelmed? Don't be! These influences aren't all bad. Being a teenager is about figuring things out and becoming your own person. Your influences can help you explore who you are!

But influences can also drive teens to be someone other than their true self. Influences can bring on feelings of being less than, empty, or inadequate. It's like, if you don't measure up, you're not good enough. Can you relate?

These feelings can cause you and your friends to get stuck in the mindset of not liking yourself for things that aren't true.

The goal of this workbook is to undo all that thinking and to help you start loving yourself for everything you are. That's what self-esteem is all about, loving yourself for who you are!

Do you want to stop feeling bad for things you think you don't have and start loving yourself for everything you are? Then you're in the right spot!

# WE HAVE A CHALLENGE FOR YOU:

**We want you to go on a quest to unlock the power-ups needed for the big level-up of higher self-esteem.**

Think of your favorite video game or movie where the hero goes on a journey. What does this look like? Usually, you need to complete a series of missions (side quests) to unlock experience and earn power-ups so you get closer to beating the final boss. This is how self-esteem works, too.

You are about to embark on a series of side quests to gain the power-ups you need to battle the final boss: Low Self-Esteem. So let's look at the Eight Power-Ups you'll need to unlock and level up!

In this workbook, we will go on a quest to unlock the eight power-ups you need to gain the big level-up of increased self-esteem. These eight power-ups are:

## SCHOOL SUCCESS

We'll start our quest where you spend a big (if not the biggest) chunk of your time: at school. What happens at school can deeply affect your self-esteem in both positive and negative ways, and we are going to explore all the ways you can navigate through school to unlock this power-up.

## HEALTHY MINDSET

We will then talk about the second power-up, having a healthy mindset. Mental health can profoundly impact you, so we will discuss positive mental health and handling stress. By the time you finish this chapter, you will be well on your way to a healthy mindset!

## POSITIVE BODY IMAGE

After caring for our minds, we will start caring for our bodies. As a teenager, you will begin to experience multiple changes in your body. We are here to talk about how to understand those changes and have high self-esteem and a positive body image in the process!

# FAMILY NAVIGATOR

Next, we will talk about your home life, where you usually spend the other most significant chunk of your time. We will talk about having a positive space and feeling fabulous around your family!

# HEALTHY RELATIONSHIPS

After we talk about where you spend most of your time, your health, and your family, we will discuss your dynamics with others (because often, other people will significantly impact your self-esteem). Here we will talk about good relationships with your peers and friends and how to begin navigating the dating world.

# SOCIAL MEDIA

Social media is a source of communication for teens, so your time spent on different sites can positively or negatively impact your self-esteem. So we'll talk about comparing yourself to others, seeing posts of all the cool stuff your friends are doing, and how to manage your use of social media so that it helps, not hurts, your self-esteem.

# BULLY MANAGEMENT

Sometimes, there will be people who try to lower your self-esteem. So we will unlock the power-up of how to face the people who seem to make things more challenging for you.

# FUTURE FORWARD

The last of the eight power-ups is facing the future with high self-esteem! You don't have to be afraid of your future, even though you can't see what it will be. By building healthy self-esteem and a positive mindset in your present, you will be well on your way to a successful future!

Along the way, pay attention when you see the words "XP Point." These XP Points are awesome bonus tips that will serve you well as you reflect on your self-esteem journey. If you've ever read a book that uses the term "Pro Tip," you will see our XP Points work the same way.

**Are you ready? Excited?
Then let's get going!
But before you start unlocking power-ups,
you must gear up to prepare for your quest.**

## Gearing Up to Start Your Quest

Before any hero starts their journey, they must do some prep work. Take your time to get ready by completing each section. Then, you will be ready to begin earning each power-up.

# Get Familiar With the Map

Take out your map and review the eight power-ups one more time. As you can see on the map, we lay out where you will find the power-ups and in what order.

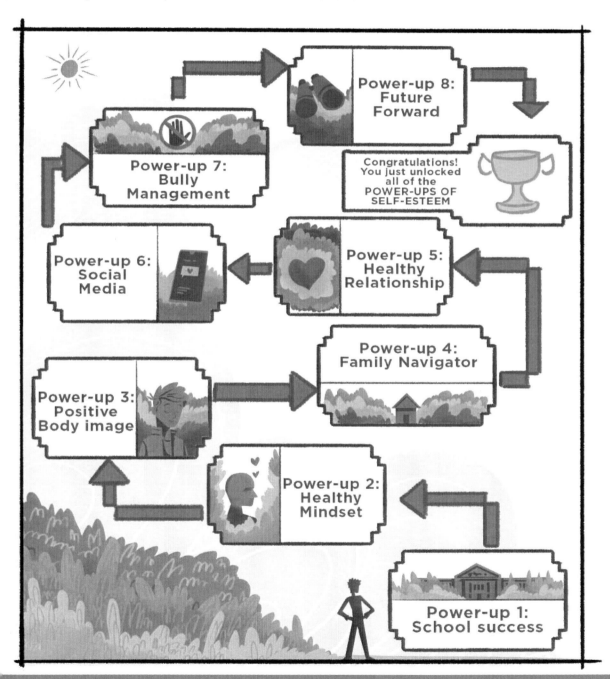

For each area, rate how much self-esteem you feel right now in that category. If that area makes you feel confident, or have high self-esteem, circle the smiley face☺. If it makes you feel down, or have low self-esteem, circle the frowning face☹. If you are unsure or feel so-so about that area, circle the face with no expression☺.

**School Success (how you feel at school)**

☹          ☺          😐

**Healthy Mindset (how you feel emotionally)**

☹          ☺          😐

**Positive Body Image (how you feel about your body)**

☹          ☺          😐

**Family Navigator (how you feel at nome)**

☹          ☺          😐

**Healthy Relationships (how you feel about friends and dating)**

☹          ☺          😐

**Social Media (how you feel when you use social media)**

☹          ☺          😐

**Bully Management (how you feel about peer pressure and standing up for yourself)**

☹          ☺          😐

**Future Forward (how you feel about the future)**

☹          ☺          😐

Take a moment to look over all your answers. Don't worry, there is no right or wrong way to answer these questions. How you feel about your self-esteem can change over time. The goal of this exercise isn't to get eight smiley faces every time. Instead, the goal is to know what areas of your life need a little more attention and kindness.

# Gather Your Team

Time to form your team and surround yourself with people who make you feel good about yourself!

First, let's make your backup team, and remember, sometimes all it takes is one great sidekick in the game to help you win.

## NAME PEOPLE WHO MAKE YOU FEEL GOOD ABOUT YOURSELF:

_____

_____

_____

_____

_____

Next to each name, write the unique way that person helps you. Your list could look like this:

## SAM IS MY BROTHER AND HE IS REALLY GOOD AT GIVING ME ADVICE ON STUFF.

## REBECCA IS MY FRIEND WHO SITS WITH ME AT LUNCH AND KEEPS ME COMPANY.

Maybe one person is good at giving advice or making you laugh when you're down. You may also have some people who are good to talk to about certain topics; like a family member you can talk about friendships with or a friend you can talk to about school. Think of this as if you are assigning a superpower to the important people in your life!

# Know Your Strengths

Before we dive into the power-ups, we'll tune into what you see as some of your strengths. Some of the topics we will discuss may make you feel many emotions. You may feel a little nervous or sad, especially if it's a difficult topic for you to talk about. To work through the sections, you'll want to have a plan in case you start to feel overwhelmed, like what are some things that make you feel happy and recharged? Maybe a video game, TV show, or a friend you can talk to.

## LIST BELOW STUFF YOU ENJOY DOING:

_____

_____

_____

_____

_____

_____

_____

_____

**Come back to this list if we discuss a topic that makes you feel negative emotions. By working through the challenges in this workbook and doing fun things to recharge, you will develop more self-esteem in each power-up quicker!**

# Have Your Catchphrase

Heard of the terms "mantra" or "affirmation?" A catchphrase in this workbook, like a mantra or affirmation, will be defined as a phrase of encouragement you can repeat to yourself. Below are some examples. Circle each of the examples you like and would try to repeat to yourself, and then there is additional room to create your own!

## I CAN DO IT.
## I CAN GET THROUGH DIFFICULT THINGS.
## I HAVE MANY STRENGTHS.
## I AM GOOD ENOUGH JUST THE WAY I AM.
## I BELIEVE IN MYSELF.

_____

_____

_____

_____

_____

_____

# Let's Begin!

Now that you've geared up and are ready to go, it's time to begin your quest and start your journey to earn the Eight Power-Ups of Self-Esteem! First, let's head to the level where you probably spend most of your time: school.

# POWER-UP 1:
# SCHOOL SUCCESS

School is where teenagers spend most of their time; because of this, your self-esteem can be impacted by what happens there. From learning new things to making friends to physical movement, many things can happen during your time at school each day. Some of these activities can be fun and engaging, while others may make you uncomfortable. No matter how you feel, know that it's normal for school to impact your feelings deeply. To begin to boost your self-esteem at school, you first need to get comfortable with your routine at school.

## Know Your Schedule and How it Makes You Feel

Your routine each day can impact your self-esteem. For example, starting your day with a class you don't like can make it tough to be positive, but you might have a class later in the day you do like going to.

Let's look at your schedule and see how your different classes impact your mood and self-esteem. In the chart below, first, fill out the different classes you have during the day and at what time. There are a few extra rows just in case your schedule differs each day.

| Class | Time | How You Feel | Likes | Dislikes |
|---|---|---|---|---|
| History | 8:45 AM-9:30 AM | Nervous | My friend is in the class with me. | It's a hard class first thing in the morning; hard to focus. |
| | | | | |
| | | | | |
| | | | | |
| | | | | |

Next, fill in how the class makes you feel. Are you happy or excited when you're in this class? Or does it make you feel nervous or frustrated? Then, list what you like about the class. Maybe you have a friend in the class or think the teacher helps you learn. Finally, write down what you don't like about the class, such as if it's difficult or you have a lot of homework for the class. There's an example in the first row, so you can understand how to fill this out.

Once you finish filling out the chart, circle which class or period in the day you enjoy the most.

Now, look at the chart again. For each class or period that does not make you feel good, is there a positive aspect or another class you can look forward to later in the day? For example, the History class may be challenging, which can make you nervous, but you have a friend in the class who you can talk to or ask for help. Another example would be if History makes you nervous, but you like the class you have after, so you can look forward to attending that class.

What positive aspects of your routine can you focus on when you must be in classes or periods you do not enjoy? Underline or highlight those. As we explore and work on strategies to improve your mindset during challenging situations, you can start by looking at the positive aspects you underlined in your schedule to focus on, especially at the beginning of your day, to put yourself in a good mindset!

# Navigating Challenging Classes

When a class does not make you feel confident, it can be challenging to know what to do. One thing we mentioned before to help you to help you is to focus on the positive aspects of the class or look forward to other, more positive parts of your day. However, it would be best if you also had strategies when you are in the middle of a class you do not enjoy. So, let's look at two different situations: when a class is boring and when a class is difficult.

# When a Class is Boring

You may feel less engaged and motivated to do your best when a class is boring. Your self-esteem can be lower because you aren't happy and involved in the class. Boredom in school is usually because of one of two reasons--you either don't like the topic, or the class is too easy.

Symptoms of boredom you may experience include:

Lack of interest in something (such as an activity, class, etc.)

Finding yourself easily distracted

Feeling restless or fidgety

We will focus only a little on when you do not like the subject in a class since it reflects more of your personal interests rather than your self-esteem. However, if you do not like a topic, try looking up real-world applications for the subject you do not enjoy. For example, did you know that historians have written plots for video games to make the games be more accurate?!

But wait a minute. How can you be restless when you are bored? Simple! When something is fun and engaging, it is easier to concentrate on it! One of the biggest reasons why boredom happens in school is because a subject may be too easy for you. On the other hand, if you feel stuck in a class where you think the things the teacher talks about are too easy, you may experience lower self-esteem because you are not experiencing new challenges or having to stretch your abilities.

Understanding what you're feeling is like leveling up your hero in a video game--the game is more interesting when your hero's power is closer to the enemy's power. If the enemy's strength is much stronger than your hero's power, the level will end in defeat quickly. And, if your hero's power is much stronger than the enemy's, the level will end very soon because of the imbalance. Classes should work the same way. It would help if you were challenging yourself, and the class material shouldn't be too hard or too easy.

## HAS THIS EVER HAPPENED TO YOU? IF SO, WRITE DOWN YOUR EXPERIENCE HERE:

_____

_____

_____

_____

_____

## What to Do

When this happens, you should practice telling others what you need. Telling others what you need is known as self-advocacy. Self-advocacy is when you stand up for yourself by expressing to others how you are feeling and what you need. In the next section, we will talk more about how to speak with your teachers about these things.

For now, check off the boxes next to the people you feel comfortable talking with if a class is boring to you:

☐ Teacher (in the boring class)

☐ Guidance Counselor

☐ Another teacher

☐ A parent or family member you live with

☐ Teacher Assistant (if you have one)

(write who they are here):

_____

# When a Class is Hard

When a class is hard, your self-esteem can be affected. For example, you may face what's known in psychology as imposter syndrome. Imposter syndrome is when you think the people around you (in this case, your classmates) know much more about a subject than you do. So when you think you shouldn't be in a class because you don't feel like you know as much as others in the class do, you may experience negative thoughts about yourself. But the truth is, almost everyone experiences this about something at some point!

## HAS THIS EVER HAPPENED TO YOU? IF SO, WRITE ABOUT IT HERE:

_____

_____

_____

Remind yourself that no one does everything perfectly, and we all sometimes feel challenged!

# What to Do

When a class is hard for you, it doesn't mean you are stupid or can't learn the topic. Read that sentence out loud to yourself. All it means is that you need the material explained differently or more practice! A great way to start getting extra help is to talk to trusted adults about what's happening. Just like with the list where you wrote down your classes and how they made you feel, find a teacher, counselor, or family member you can talk to for support if a class is too hard. Things you might ask them about are:

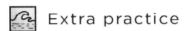 Extra practice

Time to talk with your teacher one-on-one to learn the materials differently

Finding a tutor

Resources to learn more about the topic (such as websites, books, workbooks, YouTube channels, etc.)

## Talking to Teachers and Other Adults at School

We have now mentioned a few examples of when it can be helpful to talk to an adult at school about how you feel and what you need. Sometimes, though, these conversations can be challenging to have. In this section, we will discuss two activities you can do to feel more confident when you have these discussions with adults at school!

## Talking to Teachers and Other Adults at School

Use the chart below to write down the people at school (including teachers, vice principal, principal, counselors, and other staff) who are easy to talk to on the left and difficult to talk to on the right.

# EASY TO TALK TO:

_____
_____
_____
_____

# HARD TO TALK TO:

_____
_____
_____
_____

Look at the people on the left who are easy to talk to. What makes those people easy to talk to? Maybe they are fun, or perhaps they are good listeners.

# WRITE THOSE QUALITIES BELOW:

_____
_____
_____
_____
_____
_____

Now, look at the people on the right. What makes those people challenging to talk to? Maybe you feel the person is sarcastic, or maybe they don't act like they want to listen to you.

# WRITE THOSE REASONS BELOW:

_____
_____
_____
_____
_____
_____

How can you get more of the qualities you like from people who may be harder to talk to? For example, rather than pointing out the qualities you don't like about them, try and look for positive ways to talk to them. Some examples include:

 If you don't like when someone is impatient, and won't listen, ask to set up a time to meet when they would have a few uninterrupted minutes to talk.

 If you are worried they will be sarcastic, start the conversation by saying, "I want to take this class seriously, and I need some help, please," and then explain what is going on.

 If you are worried they will interrupt you, try to be concise. Can you explain your situation in one or two sentences?

## WHAT ARE SOME WAYS YOU CAN TRY USING THIS STRATEGY? WRITE THOSE BELOW:

_____

_____

_____

_____

_____

_____

# Practicing Gratitude

One of the best ways to have good conversations with other people is to express gratitude. By saying things like "thank you" or "I appreciate it when...," you are acknowledging that the other person is trying to do something kind or helpful for you. Showing gratitude can boost your self-esteem. You might notice that conversations with most people go much more smoothly!

Here are some examples of how you can use gratitude to talk to adults at school:

 End every email you send with: "Thank you for your time."

 When you ask a question, say "thank you" for their answer.

 When an adult at school makes time to meet with you, you can say something like, "I appreciate you taking time to talk to me."

 Any time they offer to help, even if you don't want to do what they suggest, say, "Thank you for the offer."

## TRY IT OUT! AFTER YOU DO, WRITE DOWN WHAT YOU DID, HOW IT WENT, AND HOW YOU FELT AFTERWARD.

_____

_____

_____

# Navigating Discipline

Sometimes, you may get into trouble at school. Whether it's your teacher involving your vice principal or principal in the situation, a phone call home to your parent or guardian, or you get detention, getting in trouble can lower your self-esteem. So how do you navigate getting in trouble in a way that doesn't hurt your self-esteem?

The Answer: Turn it into a learning experience!

> Whenever you get in trouble, there is a lesson you can learn about safety, other people's feelings, being courteous, or respecting other people's boundaries. It does not mean you are a bad person.

# MATCH EACH SITUATION ON THE LEFT WITH A POSSIBLE LESSON YOU CAN LEARN ON THE RIGHT.

| | |
|---|---|
| 1) Getting detention for cutting class. | A) Getting a grade you didn't earn won't be helpful later if you need to use that skill and didn't learn it. |
| 2) Getting a call home for damaging something in the classroom. | B) Other people have to spend their money to buy what they own, and it's not kind to harm their things. |
| 3) Getting sent out of class for cursing. | C) Attendance is important; the more you miss, the harder school can become. |
| 4) Going to the principal's office for yelling at another student. | D) Even though it may be okay at home or with your friends, it isn't allowed at school, and we must respect the school's rules. |
| 5) Discipline for cheating on a test. | E) It is important to be respectful of other people, even if you disagree. You can also get an adult to help if things feel unsafe or difficult to settle. |

If you get in trouble, try to keep calm when it happens. It may make you sad or anxious, but try your best to stay calm by taking deep breaths or asking for a minute to process what's happened. By keeping calm, you can explain your side of the story more easily, which will help with self-advocacy. Remember, if you feel things are unfair, you can always talk to another adult or family member about what is happening.

(Answer Key: 1-C, 2-B, 3-D, 4-E, 5-A)

# Long Days

School usually lasts 6-8 hours, which is a big chunk of your day! When you feel tired, you can become burnt out which can lower your mood. Lower moods can also affect self-esteem. For example, if you get tired during the day or have challenges getting to school on time, review some of the self-advocacy strategies mentioned in this chapter. They can help with this, as well!

# A Quick Word on Friendships and Bullies

We will talk about friendships and bullies in later chapters, so don't worry; we didn't forget these are very big parts of your school day! They are so important that they get their own chapters. Until we get to those chapters, begin to think about what classes and times during your school day you can be around the people you like and when you face the people you do not like. Can you use the times you are around friends as something to look forward to? Can you have a friend keep you company during times when you will see people you do not like? More on this in a later chapter!

# Power-up Unlocked

Congratulations! You just unlocked Power-Up 1: School Success! In this power-up, you have learned to navigate the hours and classes during your school day, how to advocate for yourself, how to talk to the staff at school, and how to learn (and not feel bad about yourself as a person) if you get in trouble at school.

# MAP

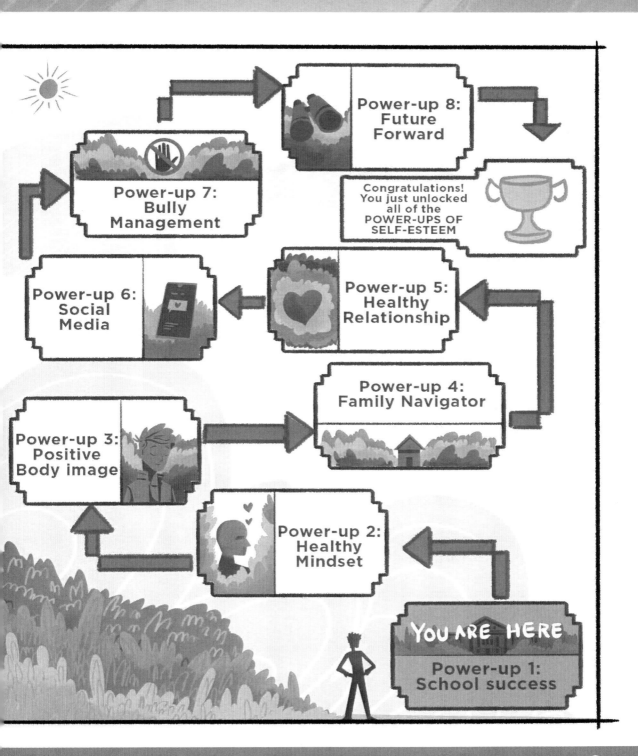

# POWER-UP 2:
# HEALTHY MINDSET

**Pop Quiz time! Three questions:**

1)At what age do you stop growing?
2)About what age do your bones develop?
3)At what age does your brain develop?

You might be surprised by the answers if you said your teenage years! While it is true that you reach your adult height and bone growth around 16-18 years old, your brain does not stop developing until you are about 25 years old.

Why is this important to know? Self-esteem is directly related to our mental health. The better our mental health, the better our self-esteem will be. And just like puberty in our physical health, mental growth and development are important, too. Therefore, it is important to nurture your mental health in your teenage years as your brain is still growing and developing.

First, we are going to talk about some of the common emotions that can impact self-esteem. Then, we will explore things you can start doing to promote positive mental health and boost self-esteem!

# Self-Doubt

Have you ever thought, "I can't do this," or "I'm not as good as other people at this?" If you have, you probably were experiencing self-doubt. Self-doubt happens when we do not believe we can do something well or think we will fail at something.

## CAN YOU NAME A TIME YOU DOUBTED YOURSELF?

_____

_____

_____

## WHAT MADE YOU DOUBT YOURSELF? WAS IT A THOUGHT, DID SOMEONE SAY SOMETHING, ETC.?

_____

_____

_____

Now let's think about ways you can think of the situation differently. Changing how you think about something is also called reframing. Reframing happens when you look at a situation in a new way. An example of reframing could be this: Instead of saying "I am bad at geometry," you could reframe your way of thinking to say "I am still learning the formulas in geometry."

## DO YOU THINK OTHER PEOPLE MAY ALSO HAVE A CHALLENGING TIME WITH THIS?

_____

_____

_____

# WHAT WOULD YOU SAY TO A FRIEND EXPERIENCING SELF-DOUBT?

_____

_____

_____

# IF YOU TRIED TO REFRAME A SITUATION IN A NEW WAY, DO YOU THINK YOU COULD THEN SEE THE SITUATION THAT NEW WAY?

_____

_____

_____

# IF YOU NEED HELP, WHO CAN YOU TALK TO? WHAT HELP WOULD YOU ASK FOR?

_____

_____

_____

Another important strategy regarding self-doubt is to say an **affirmation** when you're unsure. An affirmation is a saying you repeat to boost your self-esteem and give you confidence.

Another way to look at an affirmation
is you can think of it as a catchphrase!

Examples of affirmations for combating self-doubt are:

- I won't know unless I try.
- I am capable.
- As long as I try, that's what matters.
- I am proud of myself for trying.

## WHAT AFFIRMATION(S) CAN YOU USE WHEN YOU BEGIN TO DOUBT YOURSELF?

_____

_____

_____

_____

_____

_____

_____

_____

_____

_____

_____

_____

_____

# Strategies to Take Away Sad Feelings

Sometimes when your self-esteem is low, you feel sad. And sometimes, when you feel sad, you may have worse thoughts about yourself.

Finding things that make you feel happy again is important when you feel sad. On the next page is a giant checklist of things you can try to make yourself feel good when you are sad. Check off the ones you know help, ones you want to try or come up with ideas of your own!

- [ ] Go for a walk
- [ ] Listen to music
- [ ] Read
- [ ] Shower
- [ ] Play with a pet
- [ ] Talk to a friend
- [ ] Talk to a family member
- [ ] Drink some water
- [ ] Splash your face with cool water
- [ ] Play a game for 15 minutes
- [ ] Watch one episode of a show
- [ ] Move your body--walk, exercise, ride a bike, etc.
- [ ] Color

☐ **Write in a journal**

☐ **Do a puzzle**

☐ **Take some deep breaths**

☐ ------------------------------

☐ ------------------------------

☐ ------------------------------

☐ ------------------------------

☐ ------------------------------

☐ ------------------------------

☐ ------------------------------

☐ ------------------------------

☐ ------------------------------

Remember, if you need a few minutes to feel sad or to cry, that's okay. It would be best if you didn't cover-up, or suppress, how you feel. However, you also want to find things that will make you smile and feel better again.

# Disappointed and Hurt

Sometimes your self-esteem is impacted when you feel disappointed or hurt. Maybe you are disappointed by a test grade, which makes you feel bad about how well you can do in school. Another example might be if a friend does not want to hang out, you may feel disappointed and wonder if they are upset with you or do not like you.

When disappointment affects your self-esteem, you can do a few things. You can ask for another opportunity. For example, you could ask your teacher if there are ways to make up for the poor grade or ask your friend if there is another time that you can hang out. You can also be honest about how you feel without being angry. For example, you can talk to someone about being disappointed in your grade or let your friend know you feel disappointed that you can't hang out but would still like to later.

Fill in the blanks below:

## IF I FEEL DISAPPOINTED OR HURT, I WILL

_____

_____

_____

_____

## IF THAT DOESN'T WORK, I CAN

_____

_____

_____

_____

## WHEN I EXPERIENCE THIS I CAN TALK TO

_____

_____

_____

_____

_____

# Jealous

Jealousy is another emotion that can affect your self-esteem. Jealousy is when a person is upset because someone else has something they want. For example, you may feel jealous that a friend has the latest video game system you want, or you may be jealous if a classmate gets a higher test score than you.

Jealousy is a normal emotion to feel. It doesn't make you a bad person. When you feel jealous, you must remind yourself that everyone is different; each person will experience life differently and to accept your life as it is. Below are some examples of ways you can change jealous thoughts into accepting thoughts.

| Jealous Thought | Accepting Thought |
| --- | --- |
| "If my friend has the newest video game, so should I." | "I don't have this right now, and that's okay." |
| "I hate that my friend thinks she's smarter than me." | "She may have gotten a higher score on this test, but I tried my best, and that counts." |
| "I hate that his curfew is two hours later than mine." | "My parents may not let me stay out as late as his parents, but that's okay. I still have fun, and as I get older, my curfew may change, too." |

# CAN YOU THINK OF AN EXAMPLE OF WHEN YOU FELT JEALOUS? HOW CAN YOU TURN THE JEALOUS THOUGHT INTO AN ACCEPTING THOUGHT?

_____

_____

_____

_____

_____

_____

_____

## Anxious

Sometimes, when you have lower self-esteem, you begin to feel nervous or anxious. When that happens, it is important to return to the present moment. What does this mean? We are so glad you asked because we will break it down for you!

Usually, your brain processes your thoughts faster than what is happening at the moment. For example, your thoughts may be worried about the future or replaying things from the past. Most of the time, however, the present moment is calmer than your racing thoughts.

So how do you get back into the present moment? The best way is to engage with your senses.

## Sight

● Can you look out the window or around the room and name the objects you see?
● Can you count patterns?
● Can you look at something colorful and name all the colors?

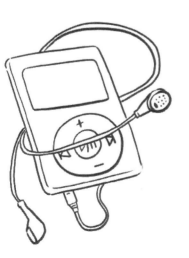

## Smell

● Do you have candles or body spray around the house you can smell?

## Touch

● Try touching things of different textures, such as clothes, towels, furniture, pets, etc. Can you describe the different textures?

## Hearing

What can you hear around you? Notice the sounds both directly in the room you are in and any noises coming from outside.
● Put on music or a show for background noise.
● Listen to a guided meditation on YouTube or your favorite mindfulness app.

### Taste

- Grab your favorite snack, eat it slowly, and try to savor the taste of each bite.
- Take a piece of chocolate and let it melt on your tongue.

## What Else You Can Do?

Now that we have talked about the different emotions you can feel that are tied to self-esteem, we are going to talk about two more strategies you can use when you feel lower self-esteem.

### Have a Self-Care Routine

What is self-care exactly? Simply put, it's when you spend time taking care of yourself. Part of the goal is to rest and recharge. The other part is to stay healthy and avoid feeling overwhelmed and tired.

How do you establish a good self-care routine? There are a few things you can do:

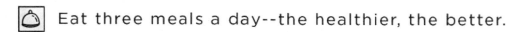 Eat three meals a day--the healthier, the better.

 Drink plenty of water.

Make sure to keep up with your hygiene (brushing and flossing teeth, showering, using deodorant, etc.)

Take breaks from your homework to rest.

 Talk about how you feel.

 Have hobbies.

If you find it hard to make time for your self-care routine, maybe you can wake up an extra 10 minutes earlier to set a good routine in the morning and then begin to get ready for bed 10 minutes earlier, so you have a routine in the evening. Another good time to practice self-care is during your lunch period or any other free time in your school schedule. You can also do this when you do your homework: take a break halfway through to recharge.

# When to seek more help

Knowing when to get more help as a teen can be challenging. Usually, your parent(s) or guardian(s) will set up doctor and health appointments for you, but sometimes, you may feel like your mental health needs more help. So what should you do then?

 First, it's important to talk to a trusted adult that knows you really well.  That might be your parent, guardian, an aunt or uncle, or a family friend.  The point is, use the wisdom of those around you to help you determine what you should do.

 Next, you can talk to a school counselor. Schools offer mental health support to students. If your family has questions or concerns about you receiving counseling, someone at your school may be able to answer their questions or concerns.

 Talk to your pediatrician. Your doctor wants to make sure you are healthy. Talk to your doctor if you do not feel well about your mental health. Your doctor can also assist you with getting the mental health assistance you need.

# Power-up Unlocked

**Congratulations!**
You have just unlocked **Power-Up 2: Healthy Mindset!**

Now that your mental health is being taken care of let's talk about your physical health.

# MAP

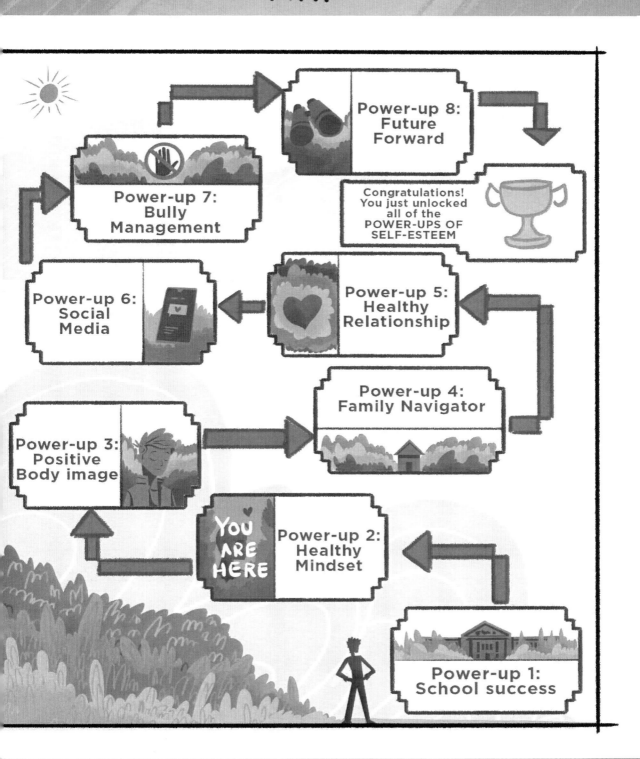

# POWER-UP 3: POSITIVE BODY IMAGE

As teens, we notice changes in our bodies. Sometimes those changes may be seeing acne for the first time, weight gain or loss, or our teeth beginning to look different. When these changes happen, they may change how we rate our self-esteem.

In this section, we will unlock the power-up of positive body image!

## Step 1: Know Your Opponent

### WHAT IS CAUSING YOU TO HAVE A LOWER BODY IMAGE? NAME THEM HERE:

_____

_____

_____

When something lowers your self-esteem, you sometimes refer to that thing as "insecurity." Having insecurity doesn't make you a bad, different, or less-than. Insecurity means you don't feel secure in your body or space!

Next, you are going to give these things a personality. Remember, whatever is making you feel less self-esteem now might be physically a part of you, but it's just a separate part of you, not who you are as a whole. So draw a character to represent everything lowering your body image. Some ideas: draw a storm-cloud creature if the thing you wrote makes you feel down. Or maybe draw a tiny creature because you will not let it take over you!

## DRAW YOUR CHARACTERS HERE:

**First, let's make your backup team (remember, sometimes all it takes is one great sidekick to win).**
**Name people who make you feel good about yourself:**

_____

_____

_____

_____

**What do your team members do?**
**What situations would you call upon each team member?**
**List them below:**

_____

_____

_____

_____

Now, let's ensure you are also getting information and support from positive places.

Social media can sometimes be supportive and fun, but at other times, it can make us feel bad about ourselves. What types of content do you follow? How do the people and content you follow affect your self-esteem? Rate the content that you follow, as a whole, below:

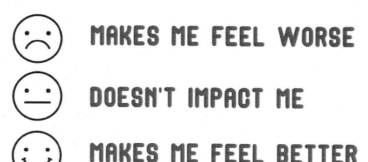

MAKES ME FEEL WORSE

DOESN'T IMPACT ME

MAKES ME FEEL BETTER

It may be time for a change if social media doesn't make you feel better. Look for content to follow which lifts you up--it could be happy or funny quote pages, entertaining distractions like a meme page, or body diversity models. Body what?! Yes! There are people on social media who are acne models, psoriasis models, oxygen mask models, and many more who display parts of their bodies that are usually stereotyped as negative. Instead, they show that every "body" is beautiful and that we should all accept our bodies for what they are!

# Step 3: Suit Up

What you wear is another important step towards having a healthy body image, so wear clothing that makes you smile, and feel comfortable and confident!

**What's your favorite style or favorite outfit you own?
Draw or describe it here:**

Positive content is out there. Time to remove or block the bad and add what makes you smile!

# WHAT ABOUT IT MAKES YOU FEEL CONFIDENT?

_____

_____

_____

_____

Finding the outfit and clothes that make you feel good will lift your mood and make you feel comfortable as you go about your day.

## Step 4: Take Action

It is time to face your opponents and express positive self-esteem for your body!

**First, name one thing about yourself that you like (it can be either part of your personality or a part of your physical appearance):**

_____

_____

**Next, name one thing about your appearance that you don't like:**

_____

_____

Now, we will talk about ways to combat negative thoughts when they pop up. We'll use more affirmations that you can say to yourself when you find your self-esteem is getting lower. Here are some examples:

It is normal to _____ (have acne/gain weight/need braces/develop stretch marks).
If I like _____ (your answer to the last questions on what you like about yourself), then I can learn to like _____(what you don't like), too.

☺ Everyone has something that makes them uncomfortable, but that doesn't make it bad.

☺ There is nothing wrong with me.

☺ As long as I am healthy, this is most important to me.

**Can you name any other affirmations that have helped you? If not, perhaps they will be something else you create or another quote that works well for you, and you can keep track of them here:**

_____

_____

_____

_____

# Step 5: Recharge and Keep Your Health Points Up

Here are some ideas for positive things you can be doing for your physical health to ease some of your concerns and help boost self-esteem:

✚ Please make sure you have regular checkups with your doctor and dentist and ask them all your questions about your body as changes happen.

〜 Stay hydrated!

☾ Get plenty of rest because this is good for your emotions and gives your body time in the evening to recharge and take care of itself.

🍎 Eat a balanced and healthy diet.

# Power-Up Unlocked

Great work! You have gained more XP points and have earned your Power-Up 3: Positive Body Image! Next, we will talk about how to navigate within your family.

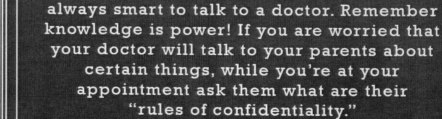

When you have concerns about your body, it is always smart to talk to a doctor. Remember knowledge is power! If you are worried that your doctor will talk to your parents about certain things, while you're at your appointment ask them what are their "rules of confidentiality."

# MAP

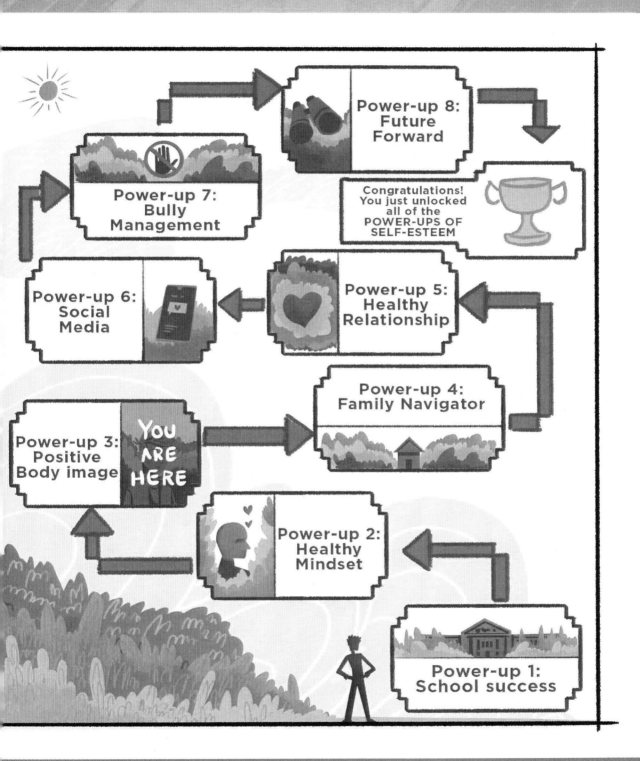

Power-up 8:
Future
Forward

Congratulations!
You just unlocked
all of the
POWER-UPS OF
SELF-ESTEEM

Power-up 7:
Bully
Management

Power-up 6:
Social
Media

Power-up 5:
Healthy
Relationship

Power-up 4:
Family Navigator

Power-up 3:
Positive
Body image

YOU
ARE
HERE

Power-up 2:
Healthy
Mindset

Power-up 1:
School success

# POWER-UP 4:
# FAMILY NAVIGATOR

Family relationships can deeply impact your self-esteem. From how your family interacts with each other to how other people talk about your family, your self-esteem can be affected--for better or worse. To start raising self-esteem in your home life, consider your family structure because no two families are the same.

## FILL OUT THE FOLLOWING CARD TO DESCRIBE WHO YOU ARE IN YOUR FAMILY.

Name: _____    Age: _____

Siblings (how many, their ages): _____    Grade: _____

_____

This makes me the (oldest/only/middle/youngest)

sibling [circle one].

We live in a (house/apartment/other) [circle one]

The adult(s) who live at home with me are:

_____

# Your Parents

The people in your family can affect how you feel about yourself, especially your parents. If they focus on your good qualities, this will help you feel good about yourself. But, if they speak harshly to you, this can hurt your self-esteem.

## HOW DO YOU FEEL WHEN YOUR PARENTS TALK TO YOU?

_____

_____

_____

## WHAT ARE SOME THINGS THAT YOUR PARENTS SAY TO YOU OFTEN?

_____

_____

_____

## IF YOU FEEL GOOD WHEN YOUR PARENTS TALK TO YOU, THAT'S GREAT! BUT, IF YOU DON'T ALWAYS FEEL THAT WAY, WHAT ARE SOME OF THE EMOTIONS YOU DO HAVE?

_____

_____

_____

# Your Siblings

Your relationship with your siblings [if you have any] can also have a huge impact on your self-esteem. Think about it: your siblings are the people you'll have a connection with all of your life.

**So, how do your siblings make you feel? Do you get along with them? Is there a sibling that you connect with better than others?**

_____

_____

_____

In this exercise, we talked about family dynamics that apply to most teens. Later on in the chapter, we'll talk more about how you can better communicate with your parents.

# Your Household

We are now going to talk more about how you feel about your current family structure, and about your familial relationships.

As you know, there are so many types of families. No particular model is better than another. Understanding your role within your family, how you currently interact with your family members and how those interactions impact your self-esteem is incredibly important to your mental health, who you are right now and who you'll become when you have your own family. But those are big topics for another book. Let's focus on self-esteem.

For this next exercise, review which family situation most fits yours and then complete the reflection questions.

# One Family. One Home

You might live in a home where all of your immediate family members are living together, ie., your parents, siblings and possibly members of your extended family. Just because you live together under one roof, it doesn't mean you get along with everyone.

## HOW WOULD YOU DESCRIBE YOUR RELATIONSHIP WITH EACH FAMILY MEMBER WHO LIVES WITH YOU?

_____

_____

_____

**Every family has their good and bad days. Write down what you like most about your family, and then write some things that are challenging.**

| Things that I Like | Things that are challenging |
|---|---|
| _____ | _____ |
| _____ | _____ |
| _____ | _____ |
| _____ | _____ |
| _____ | _____ |
| _____ | _____ |
| _____ | _____ |
| _____ | _____ |

**How would you describe the overall 'vibe' in your household?**

_____

_____

_____

**Are there any family members who are away often [because of business trips or other work related activities, attending to extended family members or volunteer roles, etc. ]**
**If yes, how does their absence impact your self-esteem?**

_____

_____

_____

# Living in Two Homes

Sometimes, teens live in more than one home. It might be because one parent lives in one house while another parent lives somewhere else, or perhaps a teen lives with their grandparents or other type of guardian for a set time.

If you spend your time between two different homes, write about the other home you live in here: ie., Is your second home very far away from your regular home? Do you have your own bedroom or do you share? Do people generally get along? Are you comfortable in both homes? Is there a home you prefer over the other?

**Siblings who live in my other home (how many, their ages):**
------------------------------

**That makes me the (oldest/only/middle/youngest) sibling in this house [circle one].**

**We live in a (house/apartment/other) [circle one]**
**The adult(s) who live in this home with me are:**
------------------------------------------------

# HOW DO YOU FEEL ABOUT LIVING IN TWO PLACES? WRITE DOWN THOSE FEELINGS HERE:

_____

_____

_____

Sometimes, living in two places can be fun since you can spend time in different areas and do different things. Other times, going back and forth between homes can be stressful and take up much of your time. And sometimes, other people, like our friends, don't always understand what it is like to live in two separate houses.

Has this happened to you? In the chart below, write about some of the things you like about living in two places on the left side and some of the challenges on the right.

**Every family has their good and bad days. Write down what you like most about your family, and then write some things that are challenging.**

| Things that I Like | Things that are challenging |
|---|---|
| _____ | _____ |
| _____ | _____ |
| _____ | _____ |
| _____ | _____ |
| _____ | _____ |
| _____ | _____ |
| _____ | _____ |
| _____ | _____ |

When you live in more than one home, it is important to stay prepared and organized to keep yourself less stressed and feeling confident.

**Can you get your things ready at least a day before you travel to your other home?**

_____

_____

_____

Lastly, if you have friends who do not understand how you live and who you live with, you do not have to give them an explanation if you don't want to. For example, you can say, "Yeah, I live with my mom some days and my dad others, and it is a lot of fun!" or "I love that I get to spend time with my grandparents during the school week, but it is also nice to spend time with just my mom on the weekends." Remember: No two families are alike!

Remember, splitting your time between more than one home isn't always bad! It means multiple adults in your life want to be there for you and take care of you. It also means that when you want to talk to an adult about something, you have more than one person to talk to or go to for advice. It only takes one person to have support, but having more than one person can be helpful, too!

# Living With a Single Parent

About one in every three kids across America live in a single-parent family (THE ANNIE E. CASEY FOUNDATION). Living with a single parent can challenge self-esteem for a few reasons. First, other kids may not understand why you live with just one parent and may ask about the other parent. Other times you may wonder about your other parent, resulting in many different emotions and feelings. In this section, we'll talk about learning how to embrace living with your one parent and lowering the negative talk about your other parent.

## WHO DO YOU LIVE WITH?

_____

_____

## HOW DO YOU FEEL ABOUT LIVING WITH ONE PARENT?

_____

_____

_____

Now, here comes a challenging but important exercise regarding your self-esteem when living with a single parent: owning your story. You do not owe your story to anyone. However, it is important to be comfortable with your story for yourself. Why? Because when you accept your own story, you can embrace and accept yourself more, which will lead to more confidence and higher self-esteem!

Say this out loud to yourself--
"No two families are alike!"

So, what is your family's story?  How did you come to live with one parent over the other?  Was there conflict and strife? How do your parents feel about each other?  And how does that impact you?  These are all questions that, although they are painful, are important to deal with and get straight in your mind.  The answers to these questions form your family's story. So let's get started.

**What do you know of the situation that caused you to live with one parent?  What questions do you still have?**

_____

_____

_____

_____

_____

_____

_____

_____

_____

_____

_____

_____

_____

_____

We will talk about how to ask your parent these questions soon, but let's end this section on a high note!

**On a scale from 1-10 how would you rate your parents' relationship ? 1= terrible, they treat each other awful, 10= they are best friends.**

_____

_____

**how does the dynamics of their relationship impact your mentally and emotionally? Try to be as honest as you can here.**

_____

_____

_____

_____

_____

_____

_____

**What do you think needs to change in your household for you to feel more secure, loved, respected, and generally happy?**

_____

_____

_____

_____

_____

_____

Do you have any other thoughts that you want to get out regarding your relationship with your parents?

**In the space below, write down some of the things you like about living with your parent. It could be the time you get to spend together, the fun places you go, or the wonderful meals they cook.**

_____

_____

_____

_____

_____

_____

Use these positive aspects of living with your parent to highlight the good! It is okay if you have questions or concerns, and we will make sure to address them. However, it is also important to embrace your life and all the positive parts of it. If you enjoy your life, it doesn't matter what other people think because it is your life--not theirs! Additionally, when we know the things that make us happy and feel good, we can try and do those things more often to bring more happiness into our lives.

### Every family is complicated.

No matter what your living situation is all families have their positives and negatives.

On the next page, there is a journal page for free-writing. Here, you can talk about your family dynamics, what you enjoy about your family, the positive and negative experiences you have faced from other people about your family, and any questions you may have for your parents.

> Remember, the reason why you live with one parent is never a reflection of who you are! It does not make you "good or bad."

# HOW DID WRITING THOSE THINGS DOWN
## FEEL FOR YOU?

_____

_____

_____

## Siblings

Remember, at the beginning of the section, we asked you if you have siblings, and if so, where are you in the birth order? That is because siblings and birth order can affect self-esteem!

Sometimes, siblings can be helpful for our self-esteem. For example, you may have one or more siblings who look out for you, keep you company, and make you laugh. You may also have one or more siblings who bully you or make you feel sad. Sometimes, a sibling can do both when they make you upset sometimes, and you get along well other times.

Or perhaps you are an only child. Being an only child can sometimes be fun because you get individual attention from your parent(s) or guardian(s). However, at other times, you may feel pressured to be a certain way, or you may want the company you see your friends have with their siblings.

## IN THE SPACE BELOW, AGAIN WRITE DOWN
## IF YOU HAVE SIBLINGS, AND IF SO, HOW MANY,
## AND YOUR BIRTH ORDER:

_____

_____

_____

Now, use the chart below to write what you like about having siblings on the left, and the things you find challenging about having siblings on the right.

| Things that I Like | Things that are challenging |
| --- | --- |
| _____ | _____ |
| _____ | _____ |
| _____ | _____ |
| _____ | _____ |
| _____ | _____ |
| _____ | _____ |
| _____ | _____ |
| _____ | _____ |
| _____ | _____ |

# Taking Time For Yourself

No matter your living situation, it is important to take time for yourself. Taking time for yourself may be challenging when you live with siblings, especially if you share a room. Make sure to take bathroom breaks, go for a walk, or get fresh air to give yourself time to collect your thoughts and feelings.

Additionally, ask yourself, "How do I feel" and "What do I need?"

Can you think of a time when you have been intentional about taking time for yourself?

**If yes, what was going on that made you feel like you needed some alone time?**

_____

_____

_____

**What did you do to 'get away'? Did you feel better after you had taken that time away?**

_____

_____

_____

**Do you feel like you managed the situation well? Is there anything that you wish you would've done differently?**

_____

_____

_____

# Conversations with Siblings

When teens need to talk to or disagree with a sibling, it is not uncommon for conversations to become arguments. So how do you have effective conversations with your siblings that boost self-esteem?

First, pick your goal of what you want to get out of the conversation. But only pick one. For example, if you want to tell your brother to be less sarcastic, stick to that topic and don't mention how messy he is. Or, if you want your sister to stop playing music so loudly, don't name-call and say she is a "loser" or another harsh term. Pick one goal, make it clear, and be kind.

Second, stick to the point and use gratitude. For example, starting a sentence with "I would appreciate it if...[then state your request]" is always a good go-to. Another thing you can do is use the good old, "please and thank you" method. Then, using the lowering the music example, you can ask, "Can you please lower your music when I need to do homework so I can focus? Thanks, it would mean a lot!"

If you notice your sibling is starting to argue with you, it is okay for you to say you are not trying to argue but are looking to resolve a problem. Lastly, if the conversation is not going anywhere, or you notice your sibling is using harsh language, it is okay to talk to an adult family member. If you do, remember not to complain about your sibling; instead, calmly explain the problem. An example might be, "I was trying to talk to her about lowering her music while I do homework, but we are having a hard time agreeing. Can you help us?"

# Conversations with Adults

Conversations with adults can sometimes seem intimidating. However, we will walk you through a step-by-step approach to having successful conversations with your parents and other adults in your family!

**Step 1:**

Timing is important. Often, adults are way busier than teens realize. They usually have many responsibilities, including being a parent, working outside the home, being a caregiver to other family members, and running a household, to name a few.

Having a serious conversation when your parent first comes home from work or when they first wake up may not have the result you are hoping for.

Instead, give your parent a few minutes to settle in or wake up. When your parent comes to talk to you, drives you somewhere, does something relaxing, or engages in a low-concentration task like sweeping, you can ask them when a good time is to talk.

Emphasize the importance of the conversation and indicate that you'll write down the topic and decided upon date and time for the talk and place it on the fridge [or another high-traffic area of your home]

## Step 2:

Your parent may stop and ask right away what's wrong, or they may do the opposite and say it is not a good time. Let's break this down. If your parent is "a worrier" and wants to talk immediately, you can ease into the conversation by giving a general sense of what is happening. For example, it may be, "I wanted to talk about something someone said to me at school," or "I have questions about the family." So you and your parent can then decide together if this is a good time to continue talking or to find a time later which is better.

If your parent is more of a 'task-oriented person, be patient. Allow your parent to finish their task and then start talking. If your parent is too busy or says it is not a good time, ask when would be a good time to talk. It is okay to advocate for yourself and explain it is important. For example, you may say something along the lines of, "Okay, when do you think we can talk? Someone upset me in school today, and I want to talk about it before I have to see them tomorrow."

## Step 3:

When you talk with your parent, practice "give and take." Clearly explain what you'd like to talk about, and then once you've explained, listen and do not interrupt. Make sure you are both taking turns talking.  This ensures that both parties feel heard and supported.

## Step 4:

Make sure you feel good about where the conversation ends. If you have any lingering questions--ask them. Or if your parent needs to do something else, talk about when you can pick up the conversation again.

## Step 5:

Use gratitude to end the conversation and give feedback! Thank your parent for talking to you. Be specific about something they did that helped you feel better or think differently about something. If they give a good piece of advice, let them know.

# Dealing with Challenging Relationships

Throughout this section we've asked you questions to get you thinking about your relationships with family members, whether they are good or bad. We've given you a few tips for how to deal with one-off situations with parents and siblings. But what do you do if, for example, your relationship with your dad has always been difficult?  What if one of your parents or siblings makes you feel down about yourself almost everyday?

First of all, we are sorry to hear about that.  It is so hard when we have challenging relationships with people that, deep down, we do love.  We are here to provide you with a few tips for improving your relationship.

# Think It Out

First let's review the situation in detail and then we can work to improve it.

Which family member do you have a challenging relationship with:

## HOW WOULD YOU DESCRIBE YOUR FEELINGS TOWARDS THE OTHER PERSON?

_____

_____

_____

Ultimately if it is a more complex situation please consider asking another trusted adult for some help arranging for counseling or mediation that might get at the deeper problem areas.

# HOW WOULD YOU DESCRIBE YOUR FEELINGS TOWARDS THEM?

_____

_____

_____

# IF YOU HAD A PERFECT RELATIONSHIP WITH THIS PERSON, WHAT WOULD THAT LOOK LIKE?

_____

_____

_____

_____

_____

_____

# IF YOU REVIEW THE LAST SEVEN DAYS, HOW MANY DAYS WERE GOOD DAYS [IE., LITTLE TO NO DISAGREEMENTS, AND PLEASANT CONVERSATIONS] AND HOW MANY WERE NOT SO GOOD DAYS?
# [IE., YOU DISAGREED AT LEAST ONCE, ETC.]

_____

_____

_____

_____

_____

_____

_____

_____

# IN THE LAST SEVEN DAYS, WHAT HAVE YOU DISAGREED ABOUT? IF YOU CAN'T THINK OF ANYTHING, THEN WRITE DOWN ANYTHING THAT YOU HAVE DISAGREED ABOUT IN THE PAST.

_____

_____

_____

_____

_____

_____

_____

_____

_____

_____

_____

_____

_____

_____

_____

_____

_____

_____

# HOW DO THOSE DISAGREEMENTS END?

_____

_____

_____

# EXPLAIN YOUR HALF OF THE DISCUSSION. WHY IS THE TOPIC IMPORTANT TO YOU? HOW DOES IT MAKE YOU FEEL? WHAT DO YOU WANT TO HAPPEN?

_____

_____

_____

# NOW FLIP THE COIN AND THINK ABOUT THE OTHER PERSON'S PERSPECTIVE. WHY DO YOU THINK THE TOPIC IS IMPORTANT TO THEM? WHAT DO THEY WANT TO HAPPEN? WHAT MIGHT THEY BE FEELING?

_____

_____

_____

Now that you have a well-rounded idea of how you feel, let's press on into some real solutions for any problems you identified.

## Step 1:

Review what you've written above. Be ready to talk about your thoughts and feelings in a positive way.

## Step 2:

Start a conversation. Make sure that you are calm and you've allowed a good amount of time between this conversation and any previous disagreements. Review Step 1 from Conversations with Adults, on page 64.

## Step 3:

Ask yourself, "have I done or said anything that would hurt this person?" And if the answer is yes, ask for forgiveness. If you are not sure if you've done anything wrong, review what you wrote about the other person's perspective of the situation.

## Step 4:

Calmly explain how a specific disagreement made you feel and why. Allow the other person some time to reflect upon what you've said. When the other person speaks, remember to listen and do not interrupt.

## Step 5:

Interpret whether you should continue the conversation based on the other person's body language, tone of voice and their words. If they seem receptive to what has been said you can continue to speak to them about the topic in a calm and gentle way. For example, you can explain why the topic that you disagreed upon is so important to you and what you'd like to see happen now.

## Step 6:

If the person has been receptive to the conversation, attempt to lay down some ground rules for how discussions will go in the future. Ensure that you allow the other person to include some rules of their own. One rule might include: neither party is allowed to leave the conversation early.

# Power-Up Unlocked

Amazing work! You did a great job of navigating your family and your family dynamics.
Congratulations!
You have earned Power-Up 4: Family Navigator!
Now, we will shift gears and talk about how to increase your self-esteem by having healthy relationships.

> You might have to have conversations like these many times before you see any long lasting improvements in your relationship. Be patient and remember this person is part of your family.

# MAP

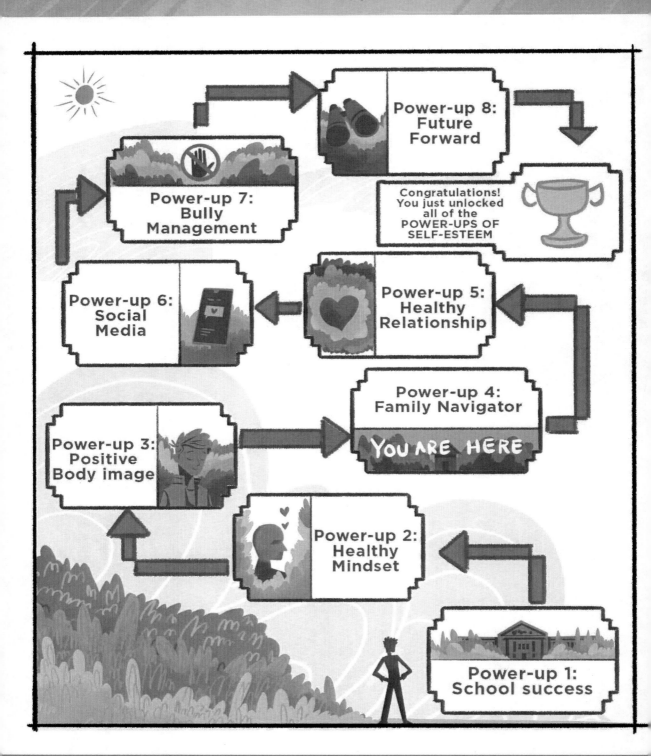

# POWER-UP 5:
# HEALTHY RELATIONSHIPS

We all form relationships with other people, whether they are good or bad. Discerning how to have healthy relationships with others is an important part of emotional and even physical development. Now, before we get into this topic, we need to be very clear what we mean by relationship; and no we are not only talking about our social media relationship status-ie., dating someone. While this is hugely important to any teen's life, there are so many more types of relationships.

A relationship is a dynamic between two people. A relationship is developed when two people interact often. It can be among family members (known as a familial relationship), among friends (a platonic friendship), or dating (a romantic relationship). As you get older, you will also develop business, or professional, relationships at your job.

As previously stated, relationships can be good or bad. For example, you and your best friend probably have a good relationship. However, if there is someone at your school who you have to see often and spend time with (such as in class), but you do not get along with, then that may be a bad relationship.

**In this power-up, when we use the term "relationship," we mean relationships in general, not a particular type. Why? Even though your relationship with your family will look very different from a dating relationship, there are tools and strategies you can use across the board!**

# Know Your Values

Knowing your values is an important, sometimes challenging, part of having good relationships. Your unique set of values will tell you what type of people you get along with easily, what you like to talk about, and how you deal with conflict between friends and family.

A value is what you decide is important in life. Different people will have different values. For example, someone in class says mean things and teases the other students. One of the students getting teased might ignore it, try and go about their day, and find something else to focus on. Another student getting teased might be more assertive and tell the person doing it to stop. These are examples of different values. In this example, the first student getting teased values not being confrontational and keeping the peace. The second student values standing up for themselves.

Values come in different forms, from how you like to spend your time, to the things that make you happy, to how you like to talk to people-. Values can even translate into hobbies! For example, if you love to read or play video games, you value books or video games as a source of what makes you happy.

You might value humor, honesty, spending time with your family, or having time for yourself. As you can see, there are many possibilities!

Now it is your turn. So let's start developing your values. Use the prompts on the next page to help you develop your values. There are also some blank spaces in case you think of anything else!

Values can change over time. Can you think of something you enjoyed a few years ago that you do not enjoy now? This change in what you enjoy is a change of values. For example: when you were younger you may have valued playing with toys, and now you may start to value spending time with friends, playing sports, or playing video games.

# WHAT ARE SOME THINGS THAT YOU VALUE WHICH MAKE YOU HAPPY?

*(This can be different people who make you happy, hobbies/activities, subjects in school, food, different places you go, spirituality or faith, etc.)*

_____

_____

_____

_____

_____

# WHAT DO YOU VALUE IN A PERSON?

*(Examples may include having humor, being a good listener, being talkative, being not too talkative, having someone with similar interests as you, etc.)*

_____

_____

_____

_____

_____

# WHAT IS IMPORTANT TO YOU?

*(Some things may be education, family, money, friendship, being hardworking, achieving your goals, etc.)*

_____

_____

_____

_____

_____

# IS THERE ANYTHING ELSE YOU CAN THINK OF OR WANT TO ADD? TO HELP YOU THINK ABOUT THIS FURTHER, FILL IN THESE BLANKS:

I value _____

_____ is very important to me.

I like people who _____

I think _____ is extremely valuable.

Remember, values are different from person to person, and because of that, there isn't a right or wrong. For example, if you value hard work and earning money, but your friend values education and school, those are both okay! Knowing your values is important because they will help you find good matches in life: relationships, jobs, and even places to live! Your values can guide you as you move through life.

Have you ever heard the phrase 'be true to yourself?' Well, this phrase essentially means, know your values, and stick with them. Base what you do and say around what you value, and you'll be true to yourself. By knowing your values and sticking to them, you will be boosting your self-esteem. You will feel confident in knowing who you are and what is important to you. Your self-esteem can be boosted when you find good matches based on your values.

This might sound confusing, but the goal isn't to be around people with the same values as you. The goal is to be around people who respect your values. At the same the goal is for you to surround yourself with people whose values you can respect. For example, let's say a teen values their faith and likes going to their place of worship (whether that's a church, synagogue, mosque, temple, etc.) This teen has two classmates at school that they talk to often. One of the classmates is not religious but is always interested in hearing about the teen's religion and their experiences at their place of worship. The other classmate, who is also not religious, does not want the teen to talk about their values and shuts them down whenever the topic comes up in their conversations.

# WHICH IS THE BETTER CHOICE OF FRIEND FOR THIS TEEN?

Answer: Probably the first friend. Just because the other classmate does not want to listen to the teen does not make them a bad person. It just means that there might be future situations that may cause you, the student who values faith, to feel let-down, discouraged and misunderstood. These feelings negatively impact self-esteem. So, when choosing friends, keep this in mind and try to make relationships with people whom we can respect and that respect us in return.

# Putting Out Your Authentic Energy

What does "putting out your authentic energy" mean? Simply put, just be you! To be authentic means to be genuine. Ok, well what does energy mean? In this statement it simply means how you carry yourself and how others will perceive you. For example, if you wave to people and smile, you may put out a social or friendly energy. If you have your headphones in a lot and look down, you may give off a quiet or reserved energy.

There isn't a "right" way to give off your energy. So what is most important is just to be yourself!

Sometimes, however, we need to push our comfort zone a little so that how we carry ourselves matches how we want others to see us. For example, you wear your headphones often because you feel too nervous to talk to others, but you still want to be social. Well, the way you are carrying yourself does not match your energy [ ie., desire to be social]. It may be challenging or scary to change this. That is why it is important to take small steps in the right direction over time. This ensures that we will be comfortable with the process. With this example, you may only keep one earphone in and take one out while you start to say hello to other people. Then, when you feel comfortable, you may walk around without headphones.

# WHAT ENERGY DO YOU THINK YOU GIVE OFF ON MOST DAYS?

_____
_____
_____
_____
_____
_____
_____

# HOW DO YOU WANT TO CARRY YOURSELF? WHAT ENERGY DO YOU WANT TO GIVE OFF?

_____
_____
_____
_____
_____
_____
_____
_____

Healthy relationships are all about maintaining and respecting values!

# HOW DOES SOMEONE WITH THAT KIND OF ENERGY LOOK? FOR EXAMPLE, DO THEY WALK WITH THEIR HEAD HELD HIGH? DO THEY TALK WITH OTHER PEOPLE? DO THEY TRY NEW THINGS?

_____

_____

_____

_____

_____

_____

_____

_____

# WHAT SMALL STEPS CAN YOU TAKE TO ENSURE YOU FEEL COMFORTABLE WHILE WORKING TOWARDS YOUR VALUES?

_____

_____

_____

_____

_____

_____

_____

_____

# Setting Boundaries

An important part of having healthy relationships with others is to set boundaries. Maybe you're wondering how setting a boundary helps you have a healthy relationship and is not limiting like most boundaries are. Setting boundaries is another way of promoting your values. Setting boundaries happens when you take a value and assert it.

## BOUNDARY SETTING DOES NOT HAVE TO BE HARD OR SCARY. IT FOLLOWS THREE SIMPLE STEPS:

### 1) Pick your boundary

What is a value that you want to assert? Here's an example. Let's say you do not like teasing and do not find it funny, but your friend keeps doing it. You know your friend isn't trying to be mean, and they are just doing it because you're friends, but you still do not like it. So your boundary might be to cut back or stop teasing.

### 2) Speak your boundary

The next step is to let other people know about your boundary.Remember: you do not need to apologize for your boundary. Instead, calmly explain the boundary, and thank them for following through on it. Using the same example, you may say to your friend, "Please do not tease me. I know you're not trying to be mean, but it makes me uncomfortable. Thank you for understanding."

### 3) Reinforce your boundaries

Sometimes people respect and understand your boundaries right away, which is great! Other times, however, people have a harder time respecting a boundary. Let's say that same friend keeps teasing you. Reinforce the boundary. You can say, "I told you I do not like teasing. Please respect that." If it keeps happening, you may say, "I feel uncomfortable, and I need a break."

# WHO ARE TRUSTED ADULTS YOU CAN TALK TO?

_____

_____

_____

_____

## A Word on Talking to Others About Conflict

Have you ever heard the expression "don't snitch?" Snitching is when you talk to someone about something else, sometimes when someone wants you to "not" talk about it. The stigma surrounding this phrase can sometimes make teens nervous to talk to other people when they are going through difficulties. So how do you know when it is okay to talk to others?

Whenever you're sticking to the facts, it is always okay to talk to a trusted adult for advice or to discuss how you feel. So let's explore this more.

Let's say you and your friend, who you are close to, get into a verbal fight. You're unsure what to do or how to improve the situation. It is perfectly okay to talk to a trusted adult about what happened and discuss how you feel or look for advice on how you can help the friendship. What isn't okay is to say things that didn't happen. So, for example, if you say your friend cursed at you, but they never actually did, don't say that.

# Knowing When to Work on Relationships vs. When to Stop

The last thing we will talk about in this power-up is knowing when to work on fixing a relationship versus when to stop being a part of it. It all boils down to--you might have guessed it--knowing your values and setting boundaries!

Every relationship and dynamic is different; ultimately, it comes down to deciding what makes you feel happy, comfortable, and confident. However, if you are really on the fence or unsure of how to decide on whether to try and work on things or to stop the relationship, you can use the following general guideline:

If you can express your values and set boundaries, if needed, and the other person wants to work on respecting your values and boundaries, you may want to give it time and work on the relationship.

You may want to end the relationship if the other person shuts you down or does not want to listen to or respect your values and boundaries.

Of course, if you feel unsafe, do not use this guideline. Instead, go to a trusted adult and let them know what is happening.

## CAN YOU THINK OF A TIME WHEN YOU WERE UNSURE WHAT TO DO ABOUT A RELATIONSHIP?

_____

_____

_____

# WHAT DID YOU DO?

_____

_____

_____

# HOW MIGHT YOU HANDLE THESE SITUATIONS MOVING FORWARD?

_____

_____

_____

## Power-Up Unlocked

Great job! You have unlocked yet another level--
**Power-Up 5: Healthy Relationships!**
We hope you feel strong and confident in your dynamics with
others! In the next power-up, we will discuss a big part of your
world—social media—and how it can help
or hurt your self-esteem.

# MAP

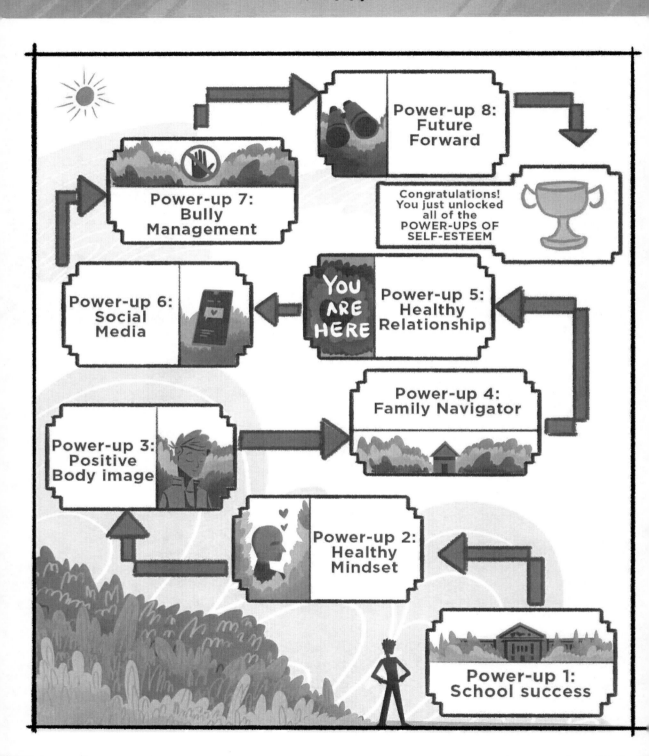

# POWER-UP 6:
## SOCIAL MEDIA

Being active on social media means you use websites or mobile apps to communicate and share things with your friends, follow celebrities, and keep up with the latest trends. You could also use it for entertainment and meet new people, sometimes in other countries.

Social media can have a positive and a negative influence on your self-esteem. Let's take a look at both of these:

**The positive influence of social media:**

You can share things you like with other people.

You can learn about diversity.

You can feel connected and supported by others.

You can find life hacks, inspiration, and "edutainment."

**The negative influence of social media:**

You measure how many people like you by how many likes you get.

You measure your self-worth by comparing yourself to what others post.

You think you always need to look and be perfect.

Someone may bully you online.

Remember how we talked a little about how social media can affect your self-esteem in Power-Up 3? Take a look again at that scale:

# HOW DOES WHAT I SEE ON SOCIAL MEDIA MAKE ME FEEL? RATE YOURSELF ON THIS SCALE.

☹ MAKES ME FEEL WORSE

😐 DOESN'T IMPACT ME

☺ MAKES ME FEEL BETTER

By thinking about how you feel when you use social media, you can begin to understand if it is helping you (being a positive influence) or hurting you (being a negative influence). So, we'll break this down and talk about each one of these ways social media can influence you.

## Positive Influences From Social Media

**You can share things you like with other people.**

We each enjoy gaming, reading, the arts, movies, etc. Social media is a good place to share these things, and you can express yourself as you talk with other people about the things you like. When you share something with others in a safe place, you are building your social skills, which can increase your self-confidence.

**You can learn about diversity and spread social awareness.**

There are billions of people on the planet, and no one is quite the same. Social media allows you to meet people from different countries and cultures and learn about the bigger world. You can also learn about social responsibility and how to be involved in a cause that matters to you. These are two ways social media can positively influence your self-esteem—you're learning about others and how to respect differences, and how you can make a positive impact by helping others.

## You can feel connected and supported by others.

Maybe there is a particular struggle that you're dealing with, like being nervous when you take tests, or you're not sure what you want to do after you graduate. Social media can provide safe groups where you can talk to others going through the same things. Some groups also offer mentors who can help talk to you about what you're struggling with. This feeling of connection can have a substantial positive influence on your self-esteem because you don't feel like you are alone.

## You can find life hacks, inspiration, and "edutainment."

Have you ever learned about using an ordinary, everyday item in a cool way? If you get a papercut, you can rub some Chapstick on it, and it won't hurt as much! Social media provides fun little tips to make your daily tasks easier, so it can boost your self-esteem because you find ways to be more efficient with your time and energy. Plus, you can share little-known facts with your friends!

Inspirational quotes and images are another great way social media can positively influence self-esteem. If you need some emotional encouragement and to be reminded that YOU CAN DO IT!, engaging with the right social media groups can be a big pick-me-up.

With many teens learning online now, social media offers a lot of "edutainment," educational videos, and online lessons that can help you learn new things. Some social media groups can help you in areas where you may struggle, like online math and science tutorials. Learning new things and improving in challenging areas can help you realize you can do something you didn't think you could, which boosts your self-esteem.

# NAME SOME OF THE GROUPS OR PEOPLE YOU FOLLOW ON SOCIAL MEDIA:

_____

_____

_____

Now, look at some of the posts you see from these groups or people and answer these questions:

1. Are the posts positive?
2. Do the posts make you feel good when you see them or read what they say?
3. Did you learn something new from the posts?
4. Did the post help you find an answer to a question you have?

# Negative Influences from Social media

**You measure how many people like you by how many likes you get.**

You get a "social feedback" element when you use social media sites and apps. This feedback can sometimes mean you feel bad about yourself if something you post on social media does not get a lot of "likes." Because there are good things that happen in your brain when you get likes on what you share, when you aren't getting the number of likes you want to get, you may feel hurt and begin to feel you don't measure up to those who earn more likes than you do.

**This kind of hurt can damage your self-esteem, so remember these things:**

 Your self-esteem is how you feel about yourself, not if others like you.
Your self-esteem means you have a good self-image and want to be yourself.
Your self-esteem is good when you respect yourself and know you are worthy.

Social media can have a positive influence on your life. When you join the right kinds of groups, look at positive and uplifting things, and learn more about how capable you are, you can know that you are using social media in a way that helps your self-esteem.

**You measure your self-worth by comparing yourself to what you see in others.**

In psychology, there is something called a Social Comparison theory. This theory says that people, especially teens, will measure their self-worth by what they see in others. For example, if you see a friend going to many different places, even different countries, you may feel like your life isn't as fun as theirs if you have to stay home. So if you see a bunch of your friends doing enjoyable things together while you have to babysit or study, you may feel like you aren't good enough to be included in the group.

These kinds of thoughts can affect your self-worth, a big part of your self-esteem, so remember these things:

 Your self-worth comes from inside you, not from what anyone else says about you.

 Your self-worth is not attached to your appearance, what you do, or what you buy.

 Your self-worth means you think well about yourself, no matter what others think.

Another thing that happens on social media is "curating." Curating means that people choose to show only the good parts of their lives and nothing that could be bad. Part of this also means that what's on social media has many filters added. So when you look at something shared on social media, you may see a picture that is touched up to look better. You may do this, too, because you want what you post to look perfect.

This is a type of inauthenticity and can harm your self-image, another significant part of your self-esteem, so remember these things:

 Your self-image is good when you like who you are inside and how you look on the outside.

 Your self-image is positive when you recognize your strengths and potential.

 Your self-image is healthy when you accept yourself completely and understand that you don't have to be perfect.

## Someone may bully you online.

Cyberbullying frequently happens on social media; some studies have shown that over 50% of teens experience online bullying at some point during their teen years. When someone is bullying another person on social media, they share thoughts and feelings that are meant to be hurtful or mean. If someone bullies you, this can make you angry, sad, and even embarrassed. You can also experience headaches and not be able to sleep well. Your schoolwork may start to suffer because you can't concentrate on your assignments or study well for your tests.

This kind of threatening behavior from another person can injure your self-esteem, so remember these important things:

 An online bully hurts your self-esteem by making you feel unloved. You can help strengthen your self-esteem by remembering that you are always worthy of being loved, no matter what anyone says.

 An online bully tries to lower your self-esteem by making you feel stupid. One way you can fight against this and keep your self-esteem strong is by remembering that you can do wonderful, creative, and intelligent things because you are not stupid.

 An online bully will also try to harm your self-esteem by making you self-conscious about your appearance. An excellent way to protect your self-esteem is to remember that you are the best YOU can be, just the way you are, on the inside and the outside.

It's not smart to say you'll stop engaging with social media sites or apps. Not using social media would mean cutting yourself off from one of the main ways you communicate with your friends. Instead of removing yourself from social media, you can find ways to use it that can help your self-esteem.

> Cyberbullying is a serious problem, and if this is happening to you, you need to reach out to someone for help, either a parent, teacher or school counselor.

A good way to measure if something on social media is helping your self-esteem is to ask yourself questions about what you see on the sites and apps you visit. Below is a chart of some things you might see on social media in the left-hand column. In the middle column, write if you think it's positive or negative. Write how it can hurt or help your self-esteem in the right-hand column. We've given you a couple of examples, and there are some blank spaces at the end, in case you think of different ones we didn't list.

| What you see on social media | Is it positive or negative? | How can it help or hurt my self-esteem? |
|---|---|---|
| A meme that shows a cat talking to a mouse about a problem | Positive | It reminds me that I can talk to my friends about my problems and that I'm not alone. |
| A mean comment | Negative | It can make me feel like I'm stupid... |
| | | |
| | | |
| | | |

If you want to use social media in positive ways which can help your self-esteem, try these things:

- Be careful with your posts – be kind, funny, and yourself!

- Join groups that post only uplifting or encouraging things.

- Follow "body-positive" influencers who are good role models.

- Join groups that may deal with heavier issues, but approach them positively, in a non-judgmental way.

- Don't compare your life to others because social media usually only lets you see good things other people post.

- Try to spend less time on social media sites and more time interacting with your friends and family face-to-face.

- Unfriend or unfollow anyone who engages in bullying, trolling, or threatens you.

# Power-Up Unlocked

Way to go! You unlocked **Power-Up 6: Social Media!** In this power-up, you have learned how social media can make you feel, how to see the difference between positive and negative things on social media, and how what you see can affect your self-esteem. Hopefully, you've also learned that your self-esteem is not based on what you see on social media but on who YOU are – a unique, extraordinary, and talented human being!

In the next power-up, we will discuss a particularly challenging issue--dealing with bullying.

# MAP

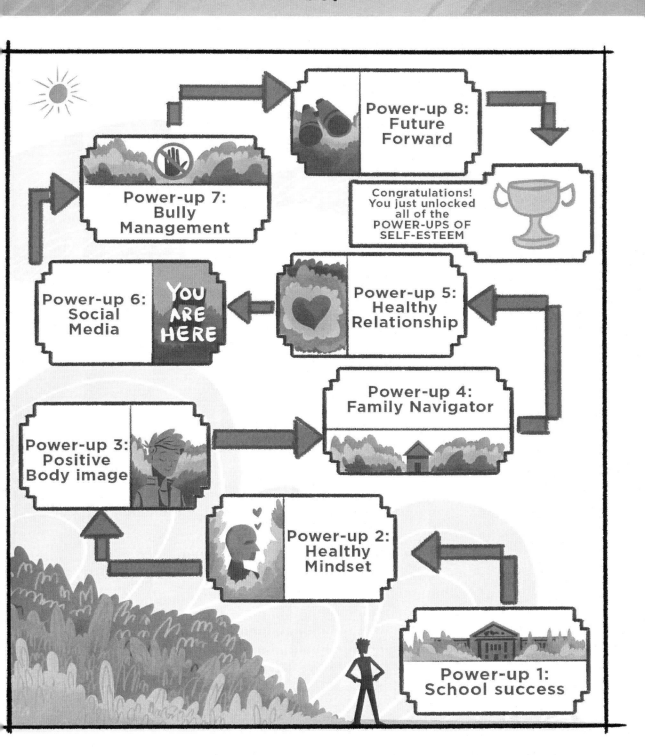

# POWER-UP 7: BULLY MANAGEMENT

Is there a particular person who bothers you often and lowers your self-esteem? You might consider this person a bully or someone who consistently bothers or harms you. This section will discuss ways to navigate bullying and keep your self-esteem high in the process!

The first step you will want to take with bullying is to talk to a trusted adult. The reason is that bullies cause harm whether it's emotionally, verbally, or physically. Because it affects your safety, you need to talk to an adult. So go back to the last power-up where you made a list of trusted adults you can speak to when you feel unsafe.

Once you have spoken to a trusted adult, you can use the following strategies in this section to help navigate the day-to-day of being around the bully.

# Assess the Situation

Dealing with a bully can sometimes feel like you do not have total control of the situation. However, when you take time to assess the situation, you create an opportunity to look for areas within your control.

## FIRST, NAME THE BULLY AND MENTION WHEN YOU NORMALLY SEE THAT PERSON.
## NAME THE BULLY OR BULLIES:

_____

_____

## WHEN DO YOU KNOW YOU WILL SEE THEM? (IN CLASSES, RECESS/GYM, LUNCH)

_____

_____

_____

## WHEN ARE OTHER TIMES YOU SOMETIMES SEE THEM? (COMING TO SCHOOL, DISMISSAL, AFTER SCHOOL ACTIVITIES, ETC.)

_____

_____

_____

Now we will talk about what has been occurring between you and the bully.

# WHAT TYPE OF BULLYING HAS BEEN HAPPENING (CIRCLE WHAT APPLIES):.

NAME-CALLING

OTHER VERBAL BULLYING

PHYSICAL

EMOTIONAL

THREATS

# WHAT HAPPENS WHEN YOU AND THE BULLY SEE EACH OTHER?

_____

_____

_____

# WHAT IS THE MOST RECENT BULLYING INCIDENT, AND WHEN DID IT HAPPEN?

_____

_____

_____

# HOW DOES THIS MAKE YOU FEEL?

_____

_____

_____

It is important to assess how you feel, accept how you feel, and say it is okay to feel that way.

# Advocate for Yourself

A big part of bully management is advocating for yourself, which means having good self-esteem. It is important to stand up for yourself by asserting how you feel and that you will not accept the bullying. While it depends on the situation, usually advocating for yourself looks like letting adults know what is going on and telling them that you need help navigating being around the bully.

Sometimes, however, you may find you face the bully in a space when an adult isn't there. Face-to-face contact with the bully may be in a restroom or outside the school building. So, how can you safely assert yourself there?

Stay calm. Showing you are staying calm can help prevent escalating the other person. Take a deep breath and stand your ground--literally.

Next, calmly explain you do not want to speak, and you can say, "I do not want to have any conflict right now; I just want to get back to class."

If that doesn't work, say an adult is waiting for you. Say your teacher or parent is waiting, depending on the situation. If you have cell phone access and can use it, you can even call a trusted adult. Simply saying an adult is waiting for you may be enough.

Make your way to the door, try to get to an open and public space, or be near the exit.

If things escalate, report what happens as soon as you can. Advocating for yourself sooner rather than later will help give you confidence that you are doing what's in your control.

# Remind Yourself of Your Worth

Often, bullies say and do the things they do because they want to lower your self-esteem. So why would someone do that? The truth is, it's complicated, and it is different for every person. Here are three possible reasons.

1. Sometimes, bullies have bad things going on in their own life; bullying others is how they deal with it. There is a saying that "hurt people hurt people," which could be what is happening in the bully's life.

2. Other times, they don't feel good about themselves, so they try to make others feel bad.

3. Others may want to feel in control and powerful by controlling other people.

However the bully in your life is bothering you, remember that just because one person is saying things about you or doing them to you does not make them true or right.

It is important to remind yourself how important you are and of your worth when this happens. To practice this, below are five statements a bully may make on the left. Your goal is to match each of these statements with positive self-talk on the right you can say to counter the bully talk.

| | |
|---|---|
| 1) "You're a loser!" | A) "I am proud of my identity and traditions." |
| 2) "You're stupid!" | B) "I am intelligent and capable." |
| 3) A bully calls you a mean name/curse word | C) "I have a lot to offer." |
| 4) A bully insults how you look | D) "That language is not true and unnecessary." |
| 5) A bully makes fun of your culture | E) "I am beautiful just as I am." |

Answer Key: 1-C; 2-B; 3-D; 4-E; 5-A

What matters most is how you think of yourself. After all, you live with yourself your entire life, so what you think is the most important!

# WHAT POSITIVE SELF-TALK CAN YOU USE WHEN A BULLY TALKS NEGATIVELY TO YOU?

_____

_____

_____

### Kindness Goes Far

When a teen gets bullied, sometimes it can get to a point where you may feel so hurt and frustrated you want to use unkind words toward others. That's one of the main ways that bullying starts in the first place! However, it is important to remember that bullying others because someone else is bullying you does not make it right.

Have you ever heard the expression "adding fuel to the fire?" It means it just gets bigger when you add more heat or fuel to a fire. So you want to put water on the fire to get it to stop!

It would help if you were around supportive friends and other people when you feel upset and discouraged. Spend time doing what brings you happiness and joy. Be kind to others to have more kindness in your life.

### When to Seek More Help

If you find that bullying affects your mental health, know that's normal. That can happen to a lot of people who experience bullying. When it does happen, however, you want to make sure you take steps to care for your mental health.

If you notice your mood lowering, talk to a trusted adult. A trusted adult can be a counselor at your school who can help facilitate treatment.

# Power-Up Unlocked

Great work! You have now unlocked
**Power-Up 7: Bully Management**.
We have touched on many topics related to self-esteem,
but our journey is not over yet!
We still have one more power-up to unlock!

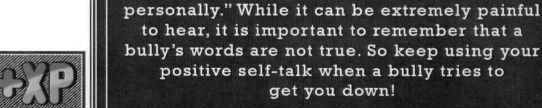

We are practicing "how not to take things personally." While it can be extremely painful to hear, it is important to remember that a bully's words are not true. So keep using your positive self-talk when a bully tries to get you down!

# MAP

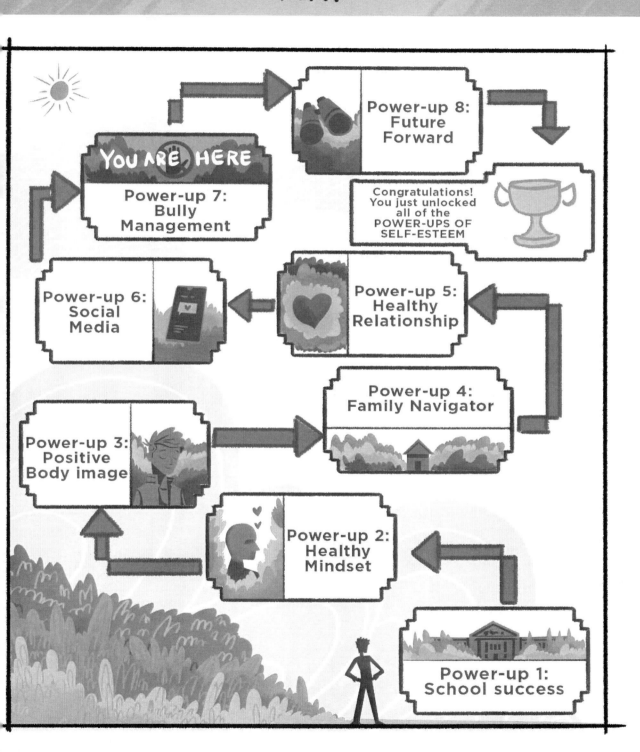

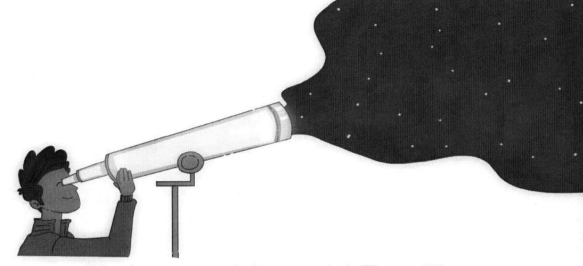

# POWER-UP 8: FUTURE FORWARD

You did it! You are at the last power-up! Great job!

In this section, we will talk about something that isn't happening quite yet: the future.

## HOW DO YOU FEEL ABOUT THE FUTURE? WRITE DOWN YOUR THOUGHTS:

_____

_____

_____

For some, the future is exciting. For others, it can be scary or intimidating. So, we will talk about ways to get excited about the future and make plans that make you happy!

# Affirming the Future

Sometimes the future may seem rather overwhelming, especially if things right now in the present moment aren't going as well as you would like. However, the present does not reflect how the future will be. It would be best if you said kind words to yourself about the future so you feel confident to move forward. Examples of affirmations about the future include:

*Tomorrow is another day.*

*I can work hard to improve my future.*

*Things right now are tough, but that doesn't mean they will always be tough.*

*I can help make my future happy.*

## WHAT AFFIRMATIONS CAN YOU USE? WRITE DOWN THE ONES ABOVE THAT YOU LIKE, AND MAKE YOUR OWN!

_____

_____

_____

Embracing the future can be tough because it is both unknown and usually involves change. Here are some affirmations you can use for the unknown changes that your future may bring:

*Just because the future is unknown doesn't mean it is scary.*

*The unknown can be a fun surprise!*

*Changes can be hard to adjust to, but that doesn't mean I won't.*

*Change means new, not bad.*

# Making Plans

A great way to make the future more exciting is to make plans for your future. It doesn't mean you have to know and plan everything now. Quite the opposite! As time goes on, your plans and goals may change, and that's perfectly okay. Making plans is to get the ball rolling and to head in a direction. Then, if you do not enjoy what you are doing, you can change from there.

Let's start small. Let's talk about this coming week.

## WHAT ARE THREE THINGS YOU WANT TO DO IN THE NEXT WEEK? REMEMBER, SINCE IT IS NOT A LOT OF TIME, YOUR GOALS SHOULD BE PRETTY EASY TO COMPLETE.

**{Examples may include talking to a friend, getting ice cream, playing a game, or starting a new book.}**

_____

_____

_____

_____

_____

How things are now is not how they will always be. Even if things are happy in the present moment, things will probably change, but it does not have to change for the worse! For example, when you were younger, you were probably happy to play with toys for younger kids. Today, you do different things to make you happy. But, as things change, what can you look forward to as you get older?

**How did that feel to make those goals? Circle one:**

**EASY**

**SO—SO**

**HARD**

If you circled easily, you may want to go on to the next activity immediately. If you selected so-so or hard, you might want to practice this activity a few more times over the next few weeks until you get more comfortable with making plans for the future.

Now, we are going to make it a little more challenging. What are three things you want to do in the next year?

## WHAT ARE THREE THINGS YOU WANT TO DO IN THE NEXT YEAR?

{These goals will be either something you want to do or something you have already started and want to complete. Examples might include finishing your grade, finding a new hobby, or trying your best this sports season.}

_____

_____

_____

_____

_____

_____

_____

_____

_____

**Great job!** With this exercise we are hoping to find things that make you feel confident and excited for the future. Don't be discouraged if these goals change a bit during the year; that's normal. For example, this often happens with adults at work. They may have a work goal, and then a new project or opportunity arises, and that goal changes a little. That's okay.

Ok, one more time. Write three goals you have for when you become an adult. These goals may change a lot in the next few years as you transition from being a teen to a young adult to being an adult, and that's okay! These goals you set will match what you value and how you feel right now. Who knows? Maybe these goals will be the same years from now!

**Examples of these goals may be the type of career you want, if you want to get married, if you want children, or what area (big city, suburb, rural, etc.) you would like to live in.**

_____

_____

_____

_____

# HOW ARE YOU FEELING ABOUT THE FUTURE, NOW?

_____

_____

_____

_____

_____

_____

If you are a little nervous or overwhelmed, go back to the affirmations section to help you unwind and feel ready for the next steps.

# Being Comfortable with the Unknown

As we talked about with affirmations, the future has its unknowns. However, not everything has to be unknown. So, for example, you can control how you handle the unknown, and how you think about it. So let's get comfortable!

What are some things that make you feel relaxed or maybe even confident? Perhaps it is music, going out, playing sports, doing puzzles, or writing.

## NAME THREE THINGS YOU ENJOY DOING?

_____

_____

_____

Next, put two asterisks (**) next to the one above that makes you feel the best. Then, put one asterisk (*) next to what makes you feel the second best.

**Now, fill in the following mad-lib style paragraph below!**

When I feel nervous about the future, there is a lot I can do to relax. First, I will try _____ (insert what you put ** next to). Then, I can also try _____ (insert what you put * next to). If I want to try something else or something different, then I can _____ (insert the strategy above with no asterisk). I can also remind myself of my affirmations. Three affirmations I can say to myself are _____ (pick one affirmation), _____ (pick another affirmation), and _____ (pick another affirmation). Even if the future is unknown, I can handle it!

**Great work!**

# Acceptance

The last important concept about looking forward to the future is accepting or embracing what happens, or what is called radical acceptance. Radical acceptance is when you embrace whatever is happening. Think of it like the expression, "it is what it is." The future will hopefully be more pleasant than unpleasant, but whatever happens, it is important to say, "Okay, this is happening, and I can handle it." You don't have to like what is happening now, but by accepting it instead of resisting it, you will be able to find ways within your power to control what is happening and make the situation better.
For example, say you fail an important exam down the road. If you were resistant you would yell at the teacher or person who monitored your exam and demand a change in the grade. Radical acceptance says, "Okay, I didn't get what I wanted this time. I can't change this moment, but I can do what is in my control in the future." Perhaps, using this example, you will schedule another exam, study, and do much better the second time!

Acceptance isn't about not doing anything about a situation. Acceptance is about knowing what you cannot change and finding opportunities in your control to focus on instead.

**To conclude this section, color in the following:**

# I ACCEPT WHAT IS OUT OF MY CONTROL, AND I WILL LOOK FOR THINGS THAT ARE IN MY CONTROL INSTEAD.

## Power-Up Unlocked

**Congratulations! You just unlocked the last Power-Up: Future Forward! Great job! Your future does indeed look bright!**

# MAP

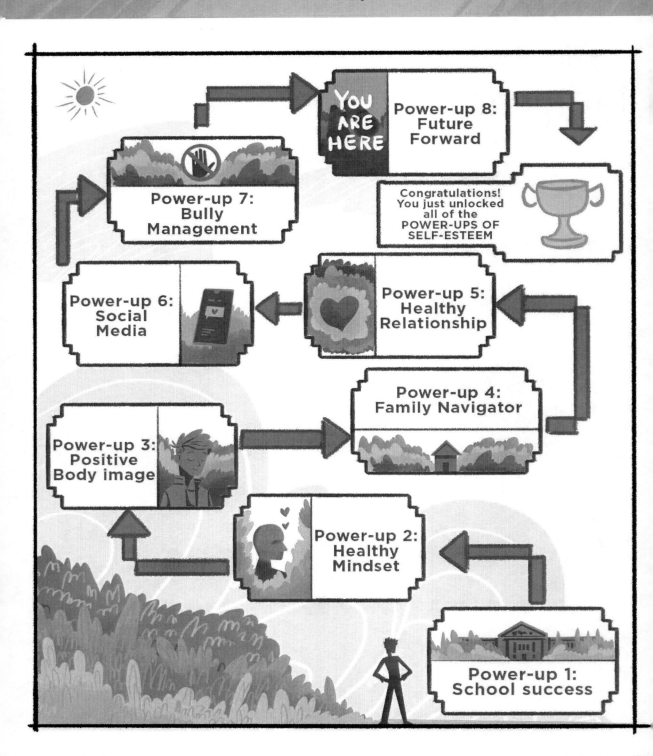

# A FINAL WORD:
# THE IMPORTANCE OF
# SELF-COMPASSION

We've discussed many areas in your life that can affect your self-esteem. Each of these areas has internal or external factors that contribute to how you see, feel, and think about yourself and how you feel your life is going–your self-esteem.

With so many different areas affecting you and your self-esteem, it can be easy to become overwhelmed with trying to manage them. Your day is full of expectations from other people–teachers, parents, friends, siblings. It can be hard or even impossible to do everything right and make everyone happy.

This kind of thinking, sometimes called negative self-talk, can hurt your self-esteem. When you speak to yourself in a way that is unkind or hurtful, you are increasing the stress hormone in your body called cortisol. If this happens too much, that cortisol can harm your physical and mental well-being.

When you think about your family or friends, you like to think you are kind and caring towards them. Self-compassion is having the same kindness and caring towards yourself that you have for others. So, let's talk a bit more about this.

## Self-compassion is different from self-esteem.

 Self-esteem is all about how you see yourself and how much you like yourself, and it can be influenced by how you compare yourself to others, and how you perceive other people think of you

 Self-compassion is supporting and encouraging yourself, not based on what others think about you.

## Three significant parts of self-compassion are

1. You are learning to treat yourself with kindness, even when you make a mistake.

2. You accept that you are a human being and are not alone, especially when you struggle.

3. You practice mindfulness, recognizing when you are hurting instead of ignoring the pain.

Self-kindness helps you to be nice to yourself, even if you make a mistake. Self-criticism happens when you feel you are not perfect at everything you do or who you are. When you are kind to yourself, you accept that you will not always be the best at everything or have things exactly the way you want. Being kind to yourself releases you from unreasonable expectations and allows you to be favorable toward yourself.

## Be kind to yourself, even if you make a mistake.

Isolation can be a cause of depression, especially among teens. You may feel like you are the only one dealing with a problem or making mistakes, but everyone around you has struggles and feelings of not being good enough.

**Accepting that you are part of a larger group of people who also deals with issues and makes mistakes will help you recognize that you are NOT alone.**

# You are not alone in this world.

Mindfulness means you can see things as they are. If you are feeling bad one day, being mindful will help you face what's making you feel bad instead of ignoring it, hoping it will go away.

Think about it this way: If you have a friend whose puppy has run away, this makes you sad. Because you feel sad about what happened to the puppy, you want to show your friend compassion. But if you ignore the sadness you feel, you are not able to also feel compassion.

Mindfulness helps you pay attention to what is happening in each moment. It allows you to notice how your body responds, what emotions you're feeling, and what thoughts you have. You must understand these three parts of your inner response system to show compassion.

## YOU CANNOT IGNORE YOUR FEELINGS AND STILL FEEL SELF-COMPASSION.

Let's try some exercises to understand these three parts of self-compassion better.

# Self-Kindness

**How do you treat a friend?**

Think about a friend you have who may say bad things about themselves.

## WRITE DOWN NEGATIVE THINGS YOU HEAR YOUR FRIENDS SAYING ABOUT THEMSELVES.

_____

_____

_____

# NOW, WRITE DOWN SOME THINGS YOU CAN SAY TO YOUR FRIEND THAT WILL HELP THEM FEEL BETTER.

_____

_____

_____

## How Do You Treat Yourself

Think about when you have said bad things about yourself.

### USING THE LINES BELOW, WRITE SOME OF THE THINGS YOU'VE SAID ABOUT YOURSELF:

_____

_____

_____

### HOW DOES THIS MAKE YOU FEEL WHEN YOU SAY OR THINK BAD THINGS ABOUT YOURSELF?

_____

_____

_____

### LOOK BACK AT HOW YOU TALKED TO YOUR FRIEND VERSUS HOW YOU SPOKE TO YOURSELF. DO YOU SEE ANY DIFFERENCES?

_____

_____

_____

# WHY DO YOU THINK THERE ARE DIFFERENCES?

_____

_____

_____

# WHEN YOU LOOK AT HOW YOU CAN SHOW YOUR FRIEND KINDNESS, IS THERE ANYTHING YOU CAN DO TO SHOW YOURSELF THE SAME KINDNESS?

_____

_____

_____

## Need For Community

Struggle and pain in this world are genuine, and it's okay not to be okay. The big thing to remember is that you are not alone in your struggles and pain. Every human (literally everyone!) has to deal with problems during their lifetime.

There is a term for this–common humanity. Common humanity means all humans want to avoid suffering and have the same needs. Take this thought to heart. None of us are alone, because we all share so much in common. That means you don't have to isolate yourself from others. When you feel like you don't measure up or you're not perfect, remember there is nothing wrong with you. You are just like every other person on the planet!

**Let's look again at what you wrote about how you talk to yourself, in the above part, with self-kindness.**

# WHAT IS ONE OF THE BAD THINGS YOU WROTE ABOUT YOURSELF?

_____

_____

_____

_____

_____

_____

_____

# NOW, WRITE WHAT FEELINGS YOU HAVE WHEN YOU READ WHAT YOU WROTE ABOUT YOURSELF.

_____

_____

_____

_____

_____

_____

_____

Finally, try to think how a good friend might try to tell you why those bad things you wrote about yourself are not true. This friend knows you well, both the positive and not-so-positive things about you, like maybe you don't brush your teeth for a full 2 minutes each time. But this friend loves you anyway, regardless of those not-so-positive traits.

**Write yourself a letter from this friend. What would your friend say to remind you that you are an incredible human?**

**Dear** _____ **(Your Name)**

_____

_____

_____

_____

_____

_____

_____

_____

_____

_____

_____

_____

_____

_____

_____

_____

_____

_____

**Your Friend,** _____ **(Your Friend's Name)**

# Mindfulness

Being aware of your internal state of mind and what surrounds you is mindfulness. Learning to live mindfully can help you avoid bad habits because you are like an observer looking at your thoughts and emotions without judging yourself for them.

Practicing mindfulness can help you in a lot of different ways:

 It reduces your amount of stress.

It helps you to regulate your emotions.

It improves your ability to focus.

 It improves your social skills.

Here is an exercise you can practice when first learning to be more mindful.

# Mindful Observing

Wherever you are right now, try these steps for mindful observing:

1. Get a pen or pencil and some paper.
2. Make sure you are sitting down, and close your eyes.
3. Try to relax your shoulders.
4. Do box breathing (see the infographic).
5. Open your eyes.
6. Write five things you see, hear, smell, and feel.
7. Write down four more things, then three things, two things, and finally, just one thing.

**An example of what your list could look like is below.**

breathe in for 4 seconds

Hold your breathe for 4 seconds

Repeat this for 4 Times.

breathe out for 4 seconds

# I SEE

# I HEAR

# I SMELL

# I FEEL

This exercise helps you to think about the way your senses are working. As you do this, you're teaching your mind to be more observant of things around you. Over time, this practice becomes a way for you to begin observing the things inside you-your thoughts and emotions.

# Ways You Can Show Yourself Self-Compassion

There are many ways you can care for yourself. As you learn more about self-compassion, one way that will help you the most is self-care.

Self-care is a physical expression of self-compassion. Self-care means doing things that make you happy and keep you physically, emotionally, and mentally healthy.

There is a difference between self-care and self-indulgence. For example, you might be sitting on the couch, eating ice cream right out of the carton, and binge-watching a series when indulging yourself.

Being lazy is okay every once in a while; but make sure you care for yourself and consider how your current choices affect your future. In other words, if, every time you have a bad day, the choice of couch/ice cream/series is what you opt for, you could end up being a couch potato and over-eating instead of taking care of yourself mentally and physically.

So here is a list of ways you can practice self-care. There is some space at the bottom of the list for you to add some of your ideas.

# Final Thoughts

While you may still have self-doubt and criticize yourself when you make mistakes, with self-compassion, you can recognize that you are only human, making mistakes is normal, and you are not alone when you have problems or feel bad.

By practicing mindfulness, you can better understand your thoughts and feelings. Mindfulness will help you examine those thoughts and feelings, not just push them down and ignore them. Remember, your self-esteem isn't going to be at the same levels all the time, and that's okay. So you can have a bad day and still feel good about yourself.

**It's not selfish to care about yourself;
it's smart.**

# CONCLUSION

## Congratulations!

You just unlocked all of the POWER-UPS OF SELF-ESTEEM. What does this mean? You'veleveled up to earn the big superpower of self-esteem! Great job!

Before we finish up, though, here is one final XP Point:

Self-esteem may change over time. If you notice a dip in your self-esteem, it doesn't mean you have lost your power-ups. It just means you need to nurture them and boost them again.

For each area, rate how much self-esteem you feel right now in that category. If that area makes you feel confident, or have high self-esteem, circle the smiley face☺. If it makes you feel down, or have low self-esteem, circle the frowning face☹. If you are unsure or feel so-so about that area, circle the face with no expression☺.

**School Success (how you feel at school)**

☹        ☺        😐

**Healthy Mindset (how you feel emotionally)**

☹        ☺        😐

**Positive Body Image (how you feel about your body)**

☹        ☺        😐

**Family Navigator (how you feel at nome)**

☹        ☺        😐

**Healthy Relationships (how you feel about friends and dating)**

☹        ☺        😐

**Social Media (how you feel when you use social media)**

☹        ☺        😐

**Bully Management (how you feel about peer pressure and standing up for yourself)**

☹        ☺        😐

**Future Forward (how you feel about the future)**

☹        ☺        😐

# SO, WHAT HAS CHANGED?
## TAKE A LOOK AT THE EMOJIS YOU SELECTED AND EXPLAIN WHY YOU PICKED THOSE.

_____

_____

_____

_____

_____

_____

_____

_____

_____

_____

_____

_____

_____

_____

_____

_____

_____

_____

Hopefully, you are seeing improvement in your power-up areas. Now you have the strategies you need to boost your self-esteem. The best way to maintain your superpower is to continue to practice.

**Great job starting your life-long journey towards having healthy self-esteem and keeping it. -You got this!**

**Draw a version of yourself defeating your low self-esteem.**

# Glossary

**affirmations-** phrases or statements that, when you repeat them regularly (either out loud or to yourself), can shift negative thought patterns and promote positive thinking, self-esteem, and motivation.

**backup team-** a bunch of friends that you can count on to help and support you through difficult times.

**body diversity-** invites everyone to embrace the variety of the human body. This extends to bodies of all shapes, and sizes.

**common-humanity-** The idea of common humanity is that we shouldn't see our struggles and failures as personal failings that cause us to isolate ourselves from other people whom we perceive to be doing better than we are.

**edu-tainment-** entertainment, especially video games, with an educational aspect.

**family structure-** refers to the combination of relatives that comprise a family. Classification on this variable considers the presence or absence of legally married spouses or common-law partners; children; and, in the case of economic families, other relatives.

**gratitude-** the quality of being thankful; readiness to show appreciation for and to return kindness

**healthy body image-** when you accept your body and feel comfortable with it. – even when it may not match other people's ideals.

**inauthenticity-** the fact of not being what somebody claims it is or not possible to believe or rely on opposite authenticity.

**[personal] boundaries-** Personal boundaries are simply the lines we draw for ourselves in terms of our level of comfort around others.

**personality-** Personality describes the unique patterns of thoughts, feelings, and behaviors that distinguish a person from others. A product of both biology and environment, it remains fairly consistent throughout life.

**[personality] strength-** the skills and actions that a particular individual can do well

**radical acceptance-** practicing a conscious effort to acknowledge and honor difficult situations and emotions.

**reframing-**when you look at a situation in a new way.

**self-advocacy -** when you stand up for yourself by expressing to others how you are feeling and what you need

**self-compassion-**involves acting the same way towards yourself when you are having a difficult time, failing, or noticing something you don't like about yourself.

**self-esteem-** how we value and perceive ourselves. It's based on our opinions and beliefs about ourselves, which can feel difficult to change. We might also think of this as self-confidence. Your self-esteem can affect whether you: Like and value yourself as a person.

**stigma-**a mark of disgrace associated with a particular circumstance, quality, or person.

**true self or authentic self-** who you are deep down.

**values-**a person's principles or standards of behavior; one's judgment of what is important in life.

# References

E. Casey Foundation, T. A. (2022, August 1). "Child Well-Being in Single-Parent Families." The Annie E. Casey Foundation. https://www.aecf.org/blog/child-well-being-in-single-parent-families

"What Are the Signs of Healthy or Low Self-Esteem?" (2022, November 7). Verywell Mind. https://www.verywellmind.com/what-is-self-esteem-2795868

Goldman, R., & MD, A. Y. (2022, November 4). "Affirmations: What They Are and How to Use Them." EverydayHealth.com. https://www.everydayhealth.com/emotional-health/what-are-affirmations/

https://study.com/academy/lesson/self-advocacy-definition-skills.html. (n.d.). https://study.com/academy/lesson/self-advocacy-definition-skills.html

"How to Teach Self-Advocacy Skills to Teens" | (2019, October 16). Understood. https://www.understood.org/en/articles/6-tips-for-helping-your-high-schooler-learn-to-self-advocate

Erban (Ed.). (2023, March 23). "What Is Imposter Syndrome And How To Overcome It" Better Help. Retrieved March 29, 2023, https://www.betterhelp.com/advice/careers/what-is-imposter-syndrome-and-how-to-overcome-it/?utm_source=AdWords&utm_medium=Search_PPC_c&utm_term=PerformanceMax&utm_content=&network=x&placement=&target=&matchtype=&utm_campaign=17990185911&ad_type=responsive_pmax&adposition=&kwd_id=&gclid=CjOKCQjww4-hBhCtARIsAC9gR3b2ar7ixnoqfdfwMnZPBy15AhSFVykL2I-IO-u5R2yoLXDx29dvqTAaAs9nEALw_wcB

Staff, M. (2022, September 21). "How to Practice Gratitude - Mindful." Mindful. https://www.mindful.org/an-introduction-to-mindful-gratitude/
I

"Why Self-Esteem Is Important for Mental Health" | NAMI: National Alliance on Mental Illness. (n.d.). W. https://www.nami.org/Blogs/NAMI-Blog/July-2016/Why-Self-Esteem -Is-Important-for-Mental-Health

"How Cognitive Reframing Works." (2022, May 4). Verywell Mind. https://www.verywellmind.com/reframing-defined-2610419

"Here's how to develop a positive body image." (2017, September 11). Kids Helpline. https://kidshelpline.com.au/teens/issues/developing-positive-body-image

Rose, K. (n.d.). "Let's Celebrate Body Diversity, Not Stigmatize It" | The Pursuit | University of Michigan  Michigan School of Public Health. https://sph.umich.edu/pursuit/2018posts/body-diversity-092518.html

"What Is Personality?" (2022, November 7). Verywell Mind. https://www.verywellmind.com/what-is-personality-2795416

"Family structure of the economic family." (n.d.). Statistics Canada https://www23.statcan.gc.ca/imdb/p3Var.pl?Function=DECI&Id=44619

"Relationships with parents and families: pre-teens and teenagers." (n.d.). Raising Children Network. https://raisingchildren.net.au/pre-teens/communicating-relationships/family-relationships/relationships-with-parents-teens

"The Psychological and Social Effects of Single Parenting in a Child's Life. "(2018, July 17). Marriage Advice - Expert Marriage Tips & Advice. https://www.marriage.com/advice/parenting/effects-of-single-parenting-in-a-childs-life/

"Siblings and Self-Esteem." (2023, March 1). Psychology Today. https://www.psychologytoday.com/ca/blog/what-would-aristotle-do/201011/siblings-and-self-esteem

Lawler, M., & PhD, S. G. (2023, March 17). "What Is Self-Care, and Why Is It So Important for Your Health?" EverydayHealth.com. https://www.everydayhealth.com/self-care/

"Improving Family Relationships With Emotional Intelligence." (2023, February 28). HelpGuide.org. https://www.helpguide.org/articles/mental-health/improving-family-relationships-with-emotional-intelligence.htm

"Talking to Your Parents or Other Adults (for Teens)" (2021, October 1)- Nemours KidsHealth. https://kidshealth.org/en/teens/talk-to-parents.html

"Personal Boundaries: Types and How to Set Them." (n.d.) Psych Central. https://psychcentral.com/lib/what-are-personal-boundaries-how-do-i-get-some

Atske, S. (2018, September 27). "A Majority of Teens Have Experienced Some Form of Cyberbullying." Pew Research Center: Internet, Science & Tech. https://www.pewresearch.org/internet/2018/09/27/a-majority-of-teens-have-experienced-some-form-of-cyberbullying/

"What Radical Acceptance Is — And Isn't. "(n.d.) | Psych Central. https://psychcentral.com/blog/what-it-really-means-to-practice-radical-acceptance

Neff, Kristin (n.d.)."Definition and Three Elements of Self Compassion "| Self-Compassion. https://self-compassion.org/the-three-elements-of-self-compassion-2

Dr. Kari Killianey. (n.d.). "Common Humanity &Mdash;" Official Site of Dr. Kari Killianey. https://dr-kari.com/my-approach/common-humanity
Staff, M. (2020, July 8). "What is Mindfulness? - Mindful." Mindful. https://www.mindful.org/what-is-mindfulness/

# Additional Resources

## Websites & Numbers to Call

**The Suicide Prevention Lifeline [USA]**
https://988lifeline.org/

**Crisis Text Line**
[USA/ Canada/ UK/ Ireland]
https://www.crisistextline.org/

**Kids Help Phone [Canada]**
1-800-668-6868

**PEER: Peer listening line for those under 25 years old.**
1-800-399-PEER

**Kids Help Line Guide to Cyberbullying**
https://kidshelpline.com.au/teens/issues/cyberbullying

**YouthLine: A Teen Crisis Helpline [USA]**
[Text 839863 or call 877-968-8491] or visit:
https://www.theyouthline.org/

**National Eating Disorders Association & Helpline**
(Text or call 800-931-2237) —

# Additional Resources

## Worksheets

**"Something About Me"**
https://positive.b-cdn.net/wp-content/uploads/2017/06/Something-About-Me.pdf

**"Things I like About Me"**
https://positive.b-cdn.net/wp-content/uploads/Things-I-Like-About-Me-Worksheet.pdf

**"Friendship Ingredients"**
https://positive.b-cdn.net/wp-content/uploads/2020/09/Friendship-Ingredients.pdf

A brief message from

# TEEN THRIVE

## Hi There!

We hope you enjoyed the book. We would love to hear your thoughts on the book. Many readers don't know how hard reviews are to come by, and how much they help authors and publishers.

**We would be incredibly grateful if you could take just 60 seconds to write a short review on Amazon, even if it's just a sentence or two!**

Visit www.teen-thrive.com/review for instructions on how to leave a review. Thank you for taking the time to share your thoughts. Every single review makes a difference to us!

## SIGNING OFF,

Teen Thrive

Made in United States
North Haven, CT
24 June 2024